Fight, Maria, Fight!

By Vince McKee

First published in 2021
Eyewear Publishing, an imprint of

Eyewear Publishing Limited,
The Black Spring Press Group Grantully Road,
Maida Vale, London W9, United Kingdom

Typeset by Subash Raghu
Graphic design by Edwin Smet

Publisher's note: the editors have left the personable writing style of the author intact, and use numbers spelled out and as symbols, interchangeably. Hell and hell are used to mean the same thing, as is earth and Earth. Single quote marks are used for brief quotes and double quote marks for speech; future editions will correct any errors we may have left in.

ISBN 978-1-913606-66-4
www.blackspringpressgroup.com

CONTENTS

Dedication	vii
Acknowledgments	ix
In Memory Of	xv
About the Author	xix
Prologue	1
Chapter One	3
Chapter Two	30
Chapter Three	65
Chapter Four	93
Chapter Five	125
Chapter Six	142
Chapter Seven	173
Chapter Eight	194
Chapter Nine	226
Chapter Ten	262
Chapter Eleven	287
Chapter Twelve	294
Epilogue	299

DEDICATION

To my mother Maria McKee:

Clearly it was your fight, spirit and belief in the Lord that pulled you through. You brought people closer to God and even if you didn't make it, I knew his work was being done through your pain. This is a story of inspiration, motivation and faith. Three things you have always instilled in my life.

ACKNOWLEDGMENTS

First and foremost, I want to thank my supportive wife, Emily, for many things. Most of all, giving birth to our two beautiful daughters, Maggie and Madelyn. They truly are the best part of our lives together. I never knew I could be as happy as I am as their father and your husband. I love you more every day and I am so proud of you. You care about others, never talk about yourself and always put others first. Those are amazing qualities and an inspiration to everyone around you to follow. I have learned over the years just how rare some of those qualities are in people, but you possess them all and I love you for it. Thank you for allowing me to have the extra time to write, announce and run my own company. I know it is not always easy putting up with my crazy hours but you do it with grace and never make me feel guilty for chasing my dream. One day it will all pay off, that I can assure you! I will always put you and the girls first, and be the best husband and father that I can be. I love you today, tomorrow and forever.

Thank you to my Lord and Savior Jesus Christ, it is through your grace that my work can be done.

Thank you to my parents Don and Maria McKee for helping me grow up the right way. I was never handed a thing and taught to work hard from a very young age. You raised me the way all kids should be raised and I will never forget that or stop being grateful for it. It didn't matter if it was a mobile phone or a car, if I wanted it, I had to come up with every penny myself. You taught me not only the value of hard work, but also the value of a dollar and to never live a life of entitlement. Those are some of the greatest lessons I have ever been taught. Everything is earned, nothing is given and I'm a better man for it.

Thank you to the amazing medical staff of Fairview Hospital ICU. You worked so hard and never gave up faith, even in the darkest moments, you kept on fighting! Nurses Amanda and Grace will forever live in my heart.

Thank you to everyone who came up to the hospital and provided the support needed in tough times. Taking time out of your day, to visit the hospital and send support, meant so much! The visiting, calling or texting was noticed.

Thank you to my sister-in-law, Abbie, for being an incredible sister-in-law and an amazing Aunt. You are what every little girl should have as an aunt. You spend time with them, make them feel special and always put your nieces first. They love you to the moon and back and I can never thank you enough.

Thank you to Libby Lombardo Ginther for setting up the food train to make sure everyone got fed once we got home from the hospital.

Thank you to my brother, Donald, for being there every step of the way by Dad's side, and in the moments when I couldn't. No one spent more time at that ICU than you. You are the greatest human being I have ever met. I know we butted heads throughout the process of what went down, but if it wasn't for you, Mom would never have made it.

Thank you to Bob and Debbie Lamb for always believing in me and seeing me for who I truly am. Thank you, Bob, for always making me feel like I am a somebody, and Debbie for laughing at my corny jokes. You may just be my number one fan, but remind me again why we watch such crappy TV as The *Bachelor*?

Thank you, Camille, Cousins Annie and Sarah for proofreading a few chapters and giving insight. That was usually Cousin Jim's job, but the Lord called him up to heaven. I miss him everyday!

Last but not least, thank you to my daughters Maggie and Madelyn Rose McKee. You make Daddy feel like a hero every single day and there is not a role I cherish more than being your Daddy. Nothing in this world beats reading to you, snuggling and watching wrestling together! You are my reason for living. As much as the pandemic sucked, being with you both 24/7 was incredible. Even when it ended, dropping you off at school, picking you up, I loved every second.

I pretend to be a writer, someone who is good with words and talking, but I will never be able to explain the love I have for my daughters and wife. It has no bounds, it has no limits.

IN MEMORY OF

There are so many people who were crucial to this story, that are no longer on this Earth. It breaks my heart. I wanted to take this time to mention them and explain their importance not only to this story, but my life.

Carrie Pell – Your beauty and kind heart will never be forgotten. From the first time I met you I knew that you were special. You had a smile that would light up the room. I think back often to my wedding day and you taking all the pictures with this huge smile on your face. I could tell quickly that wasn't a work assignment for you that day, but something you loved doing and being around. I'll never forget you, how you stepped up out of nowhere to watch the girls when we had nowhere to turn. How you became a friend to me for life and how proud you were when I got my first book published. What I will remember most about you is how much you loved being a Mother and a Grandmother. I miss you; I think about you daily and I pray for your family. Carrie, as I know you are up in heaven reading this, or even watching me type, I'm sure you already know how much you meant to my life and others. You will always be missed and loved.

Cathy Wade – If there was ever a selfless person who thought about everyone else first it was you. If I could put your heart and spirit into every living creature I would. You were so smart, and special and the world was better having you in it. Just look at the craziness of 2020 since you left it! Not a day has gone by that I have not thought about you. You gave me so much confidence. I don't have the words to explain just how much you meant to all of us. I miss you so bad and I know my parents do too. Your patience, your loving heart, just everything about you was perfect. I find peace only in the fact that you are now in heaven and pain free from cancer. I love you and I miss you!

Matt Medley – You were a mentor of mine when I first started covering sports, and I will never forget that. The night my Mom went into the ICU, you were the very first person to reach out and speak with me. The Lord took you away from us far too soon, but I truly believe in your 25 years on Earth, you accomplished more than many do in a lifetime. Miss you brother! You passed away less than 60 days after this story and I never got the chance to thank you. I take comfort in knowing that you and your Grandma are sitting courtside for every Cavaliers game moving forward. Enjoy the view!

Cousin Jim – You were by my side, every word, during the early days of my writing career. This will be the first book I cannot send you an autographed copy of. Your friendship and guidance meant the world to me! I miss your handwritten cards in the mail and talking about everything from the weather to health. I hope you are enjoying a good book and a glass of wine up in Heaven. There is no amount of money that could replace the guidance you gave me on life and literature!

Rosemarie DeLuca, my Grandma – was the sweetest human being on the face of the Earth. Her passing into Heaven was so well-deserved as she finally got to be with her mother she lost at 16 years old in 1950. Rather than trying to squeeze what she meant to me into a few paragraphs, I have posted a full tribute to her at the very end of this book as she would have deserved. Enjoy!

ABOUT THE AUTHOR

Bio

Vince McKee enjoys spending time with his beautiful wife Emily, and daughters Maggie and Madelyn. He is the Owner of KEE On Sports Media Group, a company built on the very best in sports coverage and broadcasts of High School Sports, Boxing, NPSL Soccer, Minor League Baseball, MMA, WWE and everything the sports fans of Northeast Ohio want to know about. McKee is an author of nine books, six of which have spent a considerable amount of time on the Amazon's best seller list, in genres of nonfiction sports, nonfiction religion and nonfiction inspiration.

Career highlights include:

Offering sports coverage for:

- Four UFC's
- The Calder Cup

- The MAC Championship
- All three levels of the Cleveland Indians' farm system
- The CONCACAF Gold Cup,
- The 2018 OHSAA Football & Basketball Regular Season
- The State Championship playoffs
- The CSU Vikings
- The NPSL Hank Steinbrecher Cup

Play-by-play commentator for:

- Cleveland SC of the NPSL (originally called AFC Cleveland) – May 2017 – current
- Battle in the Ballroom Boxing – May 2017 – current
- Friday Night Fights Boxing – January 2019 – current
- Cleveland Golden Gloves of Boxing (2019)
- Junior Olympics of Boxing (2019)
- The Lorain County Nightmares of the PAFL – April 2018 – current

- OHSAA sporting events all over Ohio – December 2018 – current
- Sideline reporter for the Cleveland Crunch Anniversary game – April 2019

Reporter for the Bochum Barliz baseball team from Germany

- April 2019 – present

PROLOGUE

Fight, Maria, Fight! is the story of one family's pain, passion and will to survive as their loved one clings to life. We have all heard the phrase, 'Miracles can happen every day,' but until you see one with your own eyes, you rarely believe that to be true.

In April of 2017, Maria McKee and her entire family witnessed one firsthand that will forever strengthen their faith, and the belief of everyone around them. An entire community came together for a cause that appeared hopeless until the very end.

Maria was in a coma for nearly two weeks and left for dead. It wasn't the first time in her life this had occurred and that journey is also detailed in this tale.

This book goes beyond the patient on the table. It delves further into the family, around Maria, that went through every step of hell with her. The story is told by her youngest son, me, who refused to give up hope, and created a 'Fight Maria Fight' movement that ended up being spread around the globe as the event became a national story.

At the end, everyone finds out exactly why sometimes it is, 'hell getting to Heaven' as we all look through the gate together.

CHAPTER ONE

Easter Sunday

Easter Sunday morning April 16, 2017 was finally upon us as my wife Emily and I sat back and watched the girls tear into their baskets. My oldest daughter Maggie 'The Bean' McKee, a little under four-years-old had waited patiently for weeks, knowing that the bunny was coming with plenty of treats and toys. My youngest daughter, Madelyn 'Zook' McKee, was also ready to party. She was only about seven-months-old at the time but could easily sense the excitement in the room.

It was an early start to the day because we had church at 10 a.m., and then I had to cover a National Futsal Tournament at Cleveland State University after that. The tournament was put on by Cleveland Soccer legend, Otto Orf. He had always been one of my heroes as a kid as my brother Don and I had watched him, and the rest of the vaunted Cleveland

Crunch, deliver three championships to the city of Cleveland in the mid to late nineties. The tournament not only gave me the chance to get my name out there on a national level, but also the chance to finally meet one of my sports heroes, Otto.

Through my work, writing for several news outlets and writing several books, I actually got to meet and befriend several members of that Cleveland Crunch team. However, Otto had been elusive so I was more than willing to sacrifice part of my Easter afternoon to meet the legend. We had spoken on the phone for my book *Cleveland's Finest*, so the chance to meet in person was too much to pass up.

As I watched the Bean and the Zook tear into their baskets, I told Emily, "This is the life. This is what it is all about right here! These are the moments that can never be bought." We had it rough as of late. I had lost my day job of five plus years at a local gas company, only weeks after Madelyn was born.

Though God made it right, it was scary as I waited for the ruling from the judge to fall in my favor, during that time. I got up every day and interviewed at well over 30 companies in 20 days before the money was awarded to me, to stay home. I remember being scared each one of those days too, but in the end, God made it right and my faith got me and my family through it. An enormous wrong was righted as the truth was discovered, and a blessing was given.

However, I tasted fear every single day as we waited for that ruling. A fear so intense I thought I would never have to go through that again. Little did I know, that was nothing compared to the fear that would soon be coming our way just a short while later. Only this time it wouldn't be several extra zeros getting placed into my bank account, but rather a miracle that would stop the fear.

Rip! Crack! Smash! One plastic egg after another was just one of many treasures for my little Maggie to find. Madelyn, my youngest, had no idea what was going on but she knew she liked it! My girls weren't spoiled, but they weren't lacking for love either. One thing they also had was plenty of food on the table, and hugs and kisses anytime they wanted them. The most important thing of that Easter morning, however, was the tradition instilled by my Mom's family in me many years ago. This was the main point of Easter: Jesus dying on the cross for our sins. Even at just under four, Maggie realized that and thanked Jesus several times. Madelyn just slobbered, oh the slobber!

The morning fun soon wrapped up and it was time for church. As Emily and I loaded the girls in the car, I couldn't help but notice how beautiful out it was that day. The weather was incredibly warm and it was nice to have Easter so late that year, allowing us to keep the snow gear in the closet. I stepped outside and took a deep breath of the morning air. It felt like it was something out of a book with the birds chirping and the sun sitting on the grass just right. It really did seem perfect!

So many times, in Northeast Ohio, Easter Sunday was accompanied by rain, sleet, snow or just typically lousy weather. Not on this day, it was absolutely gorgeous. In fact, it was so nice out with such clear skies, that we could see the house on fire across the street. Wait. House on fire? I bolted at the first sight of smoke as I instantly worried one of our neighbors might be in danger. Most of our street was either filled with young families or senior citizens, and this was coming from one of the senior houses.

The houses located on the opposite side of the street from us had woods in their backyards. Thus, I had thought that one of the trees somehow caught on fire and attached itself to a house. It turned out I wasn't all the way wrong; it was a garage on fire, but not from the woods. Rather, someone's compost heap had started the blaze. Odd as it seems it was totally possible and had already happened once or twice over the years.

We're lucky enough to live on such a close knitted street, and when I say close, I mean the people and their kindness. For the most part, our neighbors all got along. It only took one person to see the smoke and the fire department was quickly called. In fact, the firefighters were already on the scene by the time I bolted across the street to find out what was going on. It wasn't long before the flames were put out and calmness was restored.

Still, despite the situation being in good hands, I couldn't help but feel that was a bad omen for the day. I made sure everyone was okay before walking back to our house to help load the girls in the car for church. My adrenaline was going 100 miles an hour and I remember thinking about how much of a jolt that was to kick start the day. I had no trouble keeping my heartbeat racing the rest of the day, but that was for much different reasons.

Easter Service was held at United Church of Christ in West Park Cleveland. It was located in my old neighborhood over by Cleveland Hopkins Airport and where I went as a kid, St. Patrick's Catholic Church. I'm Catholic born and raised as well is Maggie and Madelyn. However, Emily is United Church of Christ and we had agreed to attend Christmas Eve Mass at Catholic Church and Easter at United Church of Christ. Truth be told I didn't mind it. We had gotten married there and every time

I walked in, I had pleasant flashbacks to our wedding day. We still planned on raising the girls Catholic and marriage is all about compromise at times, so it wasn't a big deal.

The service was nice and it even had a very fun Easter egg hunt for the children afterwards. I had so much fun watching Maggie run, laugh and play. Being her Daddy is one of the greatest parts of my life, then, now and forever! There was just something about that day and that moment that felt so very peaceful. Never would I have known or even feared what was about to come my family's way just a few short hours later.

After collecting enough candy filled eggs for an afternoon filled with sugar, we headed home. Normally Easter Sundays are spent with Emily's side of the family. Her mom's sister hosts a get together for everyone, and it is a nice restful day. However, this year, I was reminded that a sportswriter truly never has a real day off as the next big story, hot lead or must-see game is right around the corner. Emily understood and that is what makes her amazing. If my girls missed me, they knew I would always be home to tuck them in.

The night before was spent with my side of the family, the DeLucas. My Mom's side of the family consisted of a fleet. Mom had seven brothers and sisters, with five still living. This resulted in seventeen nephews and nieces for her and Dad, and a multitude of brother and sister in-laws. Not to mention the great nephews and nieces as well. Over fifty of us combined to have one amazing Easter Saturday night at the nursing home my Grandpa was staying at for his rehab stint from several falls.

★★★

I want to quickly backtrack for a second because this is extremely important to the rest of the story. My Mom, Maria DeLuca McKee, was the third child of eight born to my grandparents, Joe and Rosemarie DeLuca. All in all, I had six aunts, five still alive, and seven uncles on that side, six still alive, with sixteen first cousins and five second cousins. My grandfather

Joe DeLuca always preached family, and how it matters the most in life. He was right, and we always stuck together. A trait that would come in handy many times, including the days to follow.

I recall thinking to myself that Saturday night, how nice it was to see everyone, and how much I wished I saw them more than five or six times a year. As mentioned, my night job as a sportswriter comes with a lot of sacrifice; some of which is lack of time with extended family. Missing get togethers is just one of the small prices to pay when you are chasing your dream. Still, it was awesome to see everyone that night and I commented to Emily how much I wished we could see everyone much more often. I would soon get my wish to see the DeLucas more often, just not on the terms I would have hoped.

I also recall how sick my Mom looked that Saturday night. I mean, she always looked a little rough because of the years of her illness, and just the wear and tear a body can go through from fifty-plus years of countless medicine, seizures, surgeries and just normal wear and tear. But that night, I could instantly tell something was seriously wrong. However, she blamed the soreness on hours spent making food for the party. I prayed that was all that it was but could tell that it just seemed to be much more. She looked *really* bad. Pale skin, trouble breathing and just appeared to be out of it at times.

My Mom is one of the most stubborn women you'd ever meet. Too stubborn for her own good at times, but always had a heart the size of Texas made of pure gold as well. She cut hair for the homeless, gathered food for them, bathed them and just always volunteered her time at several church functions no matter what health she may have been in. Over the years she was touching lives, teaching Parish School of Religion (PSR) classes, or being a leader at Youth Group, or other various functions. She didn't know it at the time, but she was creating prayer warriors. Prayer Warriors that would soon be tasked with the gigantic responsibility of saving her life.

Emily noticed how sick my Mom was that evening as well. It was hard to focus on one thing with so many people walking around, talking and just having fun, but it wasn't hard to notice how she looked. It was concerning, not just in a son worrying about his mother type of way. To be bluntly honest, she took care of our girls twice a week while we were at work, and I feared that any energy she may have left would get expended on them when she needed to rest. She was too proud to stay home, but I could already sense we had a bubbling issue on the near horizon.

My Dad and Mom had been babysitting our girls ever since Maggie was born in 2013 during the week. They took Monday and Tuesdays; our neighbor, Bev, took Wednesdays; and Emily's parents took Thursdays and Fridays. It was the perfect solution to daycare. I mean, who wouldn't prefer their own family and close friends watching their children over strangers? My wife and children are the most important people in my life. I can't even begin to think of some stranger holding my daughters and watching them as babies. Emily and I are so incredibly lucky to have the blessing that we do when it comes to babysitters being family members and close friends.

Maggie called my Mom and Emily's Mom, 'Maga.' We have no clue where she got it from, but to hear her say it once was all it took to stick. She had grown so incredibly close to Mom. Mom and Dad built a clubhouse in their backyard for Maggie and she talked about it constantly. Mom even drew numbers and letters on the walls along with pictures of Maggie's favorite Disney characters. It was just one of those things so special you cannot even put it into words. When Madelyn got older, they made additions for her as well and they both loved it! Maggie loved both of her Magas very much! She was a blessed little girl in that aspect. Not everyone has that treasure like her, and then baby sister Madelyn had as well.

★★★

Zip, laptop packed, swish, water bottle filled, phone charged up, assignment ready! Back to reality it was as I kissed the girls goodbye, told them to behave (like Madelyn had any clue what I was saying) and headed for the door. For me Easter was over, and work was set to begin. The day job may have been a steady income with health benefits and 401K, but I was headed out the door to do what I'm truly passionate about.

It was a weird feeling. I was leaving on a holiday to go cover sports, but it was a labor of love and a sacrifice I was willing to make. I worked a day job in Fairlawn Ohio at a rubber company 45 hours a week, but it was no secret my true passion was sports writing. I had written nine published books, seven of which were on professional sports. I had met almost every living Cleveland sports legend because of it. It was a dream. I had been on TV and the radio countless times, and there were days where it just seemed like a giant fantasy that all this incredible stuff had been happening to me over the course of the last five plus years since my first book *Hero* was published. It really was a dream playing out in real life.

It's a funny thing about dream worlds sometimes though. Sometimes it only takes seconds to bring you right back to reality. As I pulled out of the driveway my mobile phone went off, it was Emily. She was very upset, screaming and crying. I had no idea why as she had agreed to let me take on this assignment weeks prior. I asked what was wrong, and she said it was Maggie and that I needed to turn around right now and come back. Considering I was only seconds removed from our driveway, it was an easy task. When I pulled back in the driveway, I ran out of the car to see what was wrong. What could possibly be so wrong, so quickly? I had just left seconds earlier!

Apparently, Maggie was upset that she didn't give me a tighter hug before I left, and stormed out the front door the second I pulled out. Emily raced after her and grabbed her before she bolted into the street. She was screaming and crying for her Daddy to come back. It was enough to make me want to quit writing right there on the spot, and never leave home again.

I had no idea where all this was coming from. Just the weekend before, I was in Buffalo covering the Ultimate Fighting Championship (UFC), the largest Mixed Martial Arts (MMA) organization on the planet and Maggie was totally fine the entire time I was gone. The UFC was fresh off being sold for 4 billion dollars, garnering plenty of press, and it was a dream come true to cover the event. As a lifelong fan of the UFC, and the fact that it was my first National Credential to cover the event, I jumped at the chance and headed to Buffalo.

As I hugged Maggie profusely, as tight as I could possibly squeeze a little girl without hurting her, I reassured her that I would be back in time for Easter desert pie later that evening. I even promised her ice cream. I mean, how hard could it be, somewhere had to be open where they sold ice cream on Easter Sunday, right? If not, I'd make it. Whatever it took for her to stop crying. She could have asked for a pot of gold at that point, and I would have dug up the Lucky Charms leprechaun.

Once again, she seemed calm and I felt comfortable enough to leave. I had been on hundreds of assignments and she had never once done that. They say sometimes children can sense when things are about to happen and try to protect you and she was.

As I once again pulled out of the driveway, I looked over at the still somewhat smoking, but put out compost heap across the street with a now char broiled grill, and just parked the car on the side of the street for a few moments. In a matter of the last 12 to 18 hours, I had seen my mom looking really sick, a near house fire across the street, and my daughter who I love more than I thought I could ever love anyone, cry her eyes out because she didn't get to hug me long enough. I was numb, I felt awful, I questioned everything and just wanted to puke. What the Hell had just happened. I went from someone ecstatic about having the chance to get paid to meet one of my idols, to a confused father trying to figure out if should I keep my commitment. I had never missed an assignment before, and this particular one was being picked up by a national website because of the enormity of the tournament. So, I decided to keep trekking along, but check in with Emily several times throughout the day, even more so than I normally do.

★★★

The tournament was the Copa North American Championship. Otto Orf had recently taken over the Ohio North Futsal organization and won the bid to host the tournament. It was huge; over 16 countries were represented and it was right in our backyard of downtown Cleveland at Cleveland State University. It was a big deal and I was stoked for it, despite the bizarre start to the day. The sport was a hybrid between traditional outdoor soccer and the faster paced indoor soccer. I didn't know much about the hybrid but was still honored to be the only media person chosen to cover it.

If I thought a small fire and screaming child was an awkward way to the start the holiday, then I truly had no clue what was coming next once I arrived on campus. Easter Sunday was about omens, one after another. Small scares, quick fixes, but the biggest and worst of the day, was about to begin on several levels. It was as if someone in heaven had a giant jigsaw puzzle of life that day and decided to start from the inside out.

As I walked into the large gymnasium, I had already called home twice to check in on Maggie and was assured she was fine and had settled down, so I took a deep breath and went into total professional mode. After all, I was being paid to be there. I needed to get my mind on the task at hand. A huge tournament and an eventual article that would likely been seen by over 100,000 people. I would typically call or text Emily only once when I got to a gig, and then text her when I was leaving to come home, but Maggie clearly had me rattled.

The first thing I noticed as I walked in the Wolstein Center at Cleveland State was a series of police officers watching the action at the door. I was shocked to see so many officers fully dressed in their gear on duty. I understood with

16 countries involved, a large amount of people in the crowd and plenty of prestige on the line, that the drama and tensions may be very high. Soccer fans here in the states may not be the most passionate, but in other countries they treat it dead serious. I also thought any form of soccer would usually bring the rowdy crowds as well. I mean, none of these countries cared about it being Easter Sunday. They were out for blood. Don't believe me? Keep reading as those soccer riots you see on ESPN from other countries can happen anywhere. Even in little old Cleveland, Ohio.

When I entered the gymnasium, Otto was initially busy breaking up a skirmish between opposing squads, so I set up camp on the sidelines and got ready to cover the action. Otto eventually walked over and we had some very nice conversation about our families, the teams in the tournaments and just life in general. I can't describe the feeling of pride and excitement meeting this man. We had spoken plenty of times over the years, but this was the first time we had actually met in-person and it was one of those things I will always treasure. As a kid, you never truly think you will meet your idols one day when you are both adults, let alone have one of those idols thank you profusely for covering their event.

After pleasantries were exchanged, it was time to get down to business. Futsal is very similar to soccer, but has two main differences that set it apart. It is played inside on a basketball court and they use a different style and texture of playing ball. It started off fun because the game is very quick moving and has plenty of goals. The playing area is so compacted and boxed in that a goalie with a strong enough arm can actually throw in a score from the opposite side of the court.

The fun of the game, the pride of covering a national tournament put on by my hero all disappeared in a blink of an eye when one of the players grabbed his private area and showed it to one of the women in the crowd after scoring. Bring sixteen nationalities under one roof, put a huge prize on the line, and then someone does something that stupid. What happened next is the type of thing you have to see to understand, but I will do my best to explain.

Clearly, the gesture and partial nudity set off the opposing team's fans, but once the woman's husband caught wind of what had just happened, all bets were off. The two teams engaged in a full out brawl. Punches thrown, people screaming and yelling and jerseys ripped. Players were ejected, fans were tossed out, it was a total rumble. Suddenly those soccer riots I saw on TV, were happening two feet from me. I was so close to the action, I had to duck a punch thrown at me. It was chaos, the likes of which WWE Promoter Vince McMahon would charge $49.99 for on Pay Per View.

After about twenty minutes of non-stop backyard brawling, cooler heads had finally prevailed and it looked as though the tournament would continue. It was at that moment that a player named Dante, from the Toronto team, came from behind and sucker-punched a man named Scotty from the Ireland team. The melee spilled over into the crowd. Literally spilling over into the crowd as Dante was running from numerous Columbians at once, who had come over to join the rumble. It was like a bar brawl in an old Western movie that you see just keep going and going as more people walk in the bar.

Dante spotted his own wife and one-year-old son in the crowd on the sidelines and ran towards them for safety. He tried jumping over them, but missed, instead landing flush on his small child and flattening the stroller, complete with baby in it. A grown man jumped onto his 1-year-old son while laying in a stroller. This all because two players on different teams, on the other side of the court decided to fight over a rude gesture.

The fact that a man was now laying on top of his child, now bloody, didn't stop the ravenous group of pissed off Columbians from piling on top of him and the baby boy. The baby was taken to hospital. It was ugly, even the women started going at it. The cops were called in, reports were filed and it took Otto 45 minutes of pleading with the local authorities not to shut down the tournament right then and there. The rest of the day would be given a zero-tolerance policy as the games resumed. The lead for my story had already been written and I was only there twenty minutes.

As the rest of the day played out, things appeared to be calming down and the games were going off without a hitch. One player did get thrown out of the championship game for spitting on another, then refused to leave the gym. Well, to say refused would be a bit inaccurate. The fact is that he couldn't leave even if he wanted to, we were locked in!

Unbeknownst to any of us during our own drama packed day was the fact that only two miles down the road, a real tragedy had just occurred, and suddenly all of our lives were in major danger. Steven Stephens had committed armed murder live on Facebook just a few streets over from the Wolstein Center. He had shot and killed a 74-year-old man while anyone with access to his Facebook page had the unfortunate ability to watch it happen.

This horrible event put everything into perspective quickly, as the magnitude of that moment outweighed anything going on at the

Futsal Tournament. As a member of the press that day, I was actually notified first along with Otto and other tournament officials that our site was now on lockdown. No one was going anywhere until the tournament was over, and a police escort could assist.

More than half of the officers who began the day working the tournament were now pulled away to assist in the Steven Stephens manhunt. I was in shock, trying to come to grips with how anyone could do something so vile. Suddenly a day that just kept serving up one chilling moment after another, found a way to get even worse.

I just wanted to get home to my girls, all three of them, Emily, the Bean and The Zook as quickly as possible. The tournament wrapped up about 90 minutes later and they still weren't ready to let people leave the building yet, so I just kept working. Writing the article, taking pictures and trying hard to keep my nerves calm. Fully realizing that a murderer could be roaming around only minutes away if not possibly hiding out somewhere in the very building we were in. It was a bone chilling feeling. Over and over in my head I just kept picturing a man walking in with a gun and shooting up the place.

After what seemed like an eternity, we were finally allowed to leave the building under police guard. We had to walk to our cars by ourselves, but we were assured that an armed police officer would be stationed close enough to intervene if need be. I ran to my car like a bat speeding out of Hell. On the way home, I never called Emily. I hadn't heard from her for several hours so my thought was that she had no clue what was going on with the murder and the fact that her husband was only minutes away from the spot it happened. If she knew, she would have been calling every few minutes urging me to leave.

I drove home glued to the local news station on my radio dial, talking about what had happened with the murder. A far cry from the normal as my radio is usually glued to sports talk radio for every mile I put on the car. I simply couldn't get over what I was hearing, and the pure magnitude of everything that occurred. One man killed an innocent man – *live* – as thousands watched? How could that happen?

★★★

Arriving home, I picked up Maggie and Madelyn and gave them both big hugs, telling them how much Daddy loved them. I wanted to hear all about their day and snuggle on the couch per our normal routine when I get home from covering games. I also had to figure out where the Hell I was going to get ice cream from on Easter Sunday night. Maggie was sure to keep me up on that promise.

However, before the trip to the 24/7 Walmart was made to secure the 'French Vanilla' ice cream, Maggie's favorite, I had one call to make. I wanted to call my parents, fill them in on the events of the day and let them know I was safe. I had mentioned the tournament to them, thought perhaps they saw some of my score updates on Facebook and realized where the tournament was held at. I called over to my parents' house and my Mom picked up the phone. She sounded awful and instantly I could tell something was seriously wrong. I told her that I was safe, and she had no idea what I was talking about. Her and Dad were so bad sick, the both of them.

I hung up the phone with my Mom a short while later and told her to rest up and I would see her in the morning to watch the kids. Hoping she would feel better by then, as Maggie and Madelyn look so forward to the days they spend with them. Little did I know that phone call may have been the final time I ever spoke with my mom.

A few hours later, I laid an ice cream filled Maggie down to bed and wrapped my arms around Emily. 'What a day,' I said, 'hopefully things get back to normal tomorrow.' Little did I know, the most chaotic Easter Sunday of my life would end up being the most calm and restful day I would have for the next twenty-two days. Pure Hell was about to arrive.

CHAPTER TWO

'Faith is the power to stand up to the madness and chaos of the physical world, while holding the position that nothing external has any authority over what heaven has in mind for you.' – Caroline Myss

It Begins

There isn't an alarm clock on planet earth that isn't obnoxious when it goes off, but the ones that siren on a Monday morning are the worst! On this day, I didn't even get that far as my Dad called before the alarm could go off. He was alerting Emily and I that he and Mom were both still sick, and wouldn't be able to watch the girls.

Emily had already left to catch The Rapid (train) to her job in downtown Cleveland, and I was still stirring. There was no way around it, we were screwed. I told my Dad not to worry about it, and just get some rest. Angels in the form of babysitters would start to appear in the coming days, but that morning, I was out of options. I had only been with my company Continental Tire in Fairlawn since January, so not even four full months. I was past the 90-day trial period, but still didn't want to run the risk of my first call off so early into my tenure. I had just lost my job of five years the previous October, so I knew to never take anything for granted.

Alas, I had no choice but to call in to work and let my supervisor, Chad, know I wouldn't be in. So, I did exactly that. He seemed to understand and I was mildly relieved. I know what you the reader are saying at this point, "what the hell does a dying mother have to do with babysitters and jobs?" Sit tight dear reader as this tale progresses it will all begin to make sense.

Continental Tire was a great company, and they had already given all their employees the prior Friday off for Good Friday. That's something no job I had ever had in the past did. However, this was not my idea of a restful four-day weekend. Instead of worrying about it, I decided to fall back on one of my favorite pastimes and lay down for one more snooze. Granted, the alarm hadn't gone off yet, but you get my point.

I couldn't even count one sheep before there was a rapping on my door, it was 77-year-old Bev from next door. Her husband Bill noticed that my parents hadn't arrived yet and that our bedroom light wasn't on. She was concerned something may be up? This was one of those times when being close with your next-door neighbors really paid off. I explained what was going on with my parents, and Bev volunteered to switch days. She told me she would watch the girls today, if my parents could pick up Wednesday that week. It sounded fair enough to me, so I said sure and got ready for the 55-minute drive to work. I called Chad on the way to work to let him know that I was coming in, and everything seemed fine.

With two parents, one was bound to be feeling better by the time I got home that night from work. I didn't think too much about it throughout the day. I kept my 100% focus on work. This job was very important, and I was still very green to the rubber industry, and battling an early learning curve. This doesn't mean that I didn't care about my parents. It simply means I didn't stress over it at all while at work that day.

At that point in my life I wasn't conditioned to worry about my parents' health every day. Sadly, that would change drastically over the coming days, weeks, months and even years. It was as if that day was the early conditioning of my brain to accept the fact that my parents were not in the best health.

You get to the point in your life where you not only worry about your kids every day, but also your parents. They spent years worrying about you and now it is you worrying about them. It may seem silly but I'm willing to bet almost everyone in their late 30s with children, and also parents in their late 60s would agree with that assessment.

It crossed my mind a few times on the drive home that day, but I was mostly anguishing over who the Cleveland Browns would select with the first pick in the National Football League (NFL) draft the next week. At moments in the drive, I couldn't help but fear coming home to bad news. The world has a lot of fears, but few are as bad as the 'unknown.'

Upon arriving home, Bev stuck around another 35 minutes explaining just how important watching the girls was to her. It made me feel good, and the second she left, Emily arrived home moments later. I told Emily I had to run out but would be right back.

I went to Giant Eagle and bought Bev some flowers and a card. I just felt like doing something nice that day. It wasn't the Lord calling me yet, but just a sense of gratitude a lot more people in this world should have. Bev saved my butt that day, and I will never forget it. A good neighbor can help make your life easier at times, a bad one can make it Hell. We were blessed to have great ones on both sides!

Our neighbors on the other side are the Lehmanns; a couple around the same age as Emily and I. Gina and Curt have three kids. The two older daughters were junior high age at the time, and the little boy, Patrick, was the same age as Maggie. They were the best of buddies and it was nice for Maggie to have a friend her age so close by. Gina would end up bailing us out of a babysitter jam more than a few times over the years.

After dinner, I called over to my parents and attempted to check in on them. No one picked up, so I kept calling until a concerned Dad picked up the phone. He had been through a lot with my Mom in over 40 years together, a story I will get to very soon, but this time seemed to be different.

Dad expressed concern and made it clear that they wouldn't be able to watch the girls tomorrow because there was no way he could leave my Mom alone. Now I was getting concerned because Mom is one tough cookie, and this was way out of character for her, and Dad for that matter. In the three plus years they had been watching Maggie, they never missed a single day. This was nerve-racking to say the least.

I had to walk the flowers and card I bought over to Bev anyways, so I knew I had no choice but to ask her for help again. I felt crappy about it because I immediately thought she was going to misconstrue the flowers for bribery to pick up an extra day, on top of the one she just took. Luckily Bev understood the jam we were in and volunteered to take on Tuesday.

Emily was willing to take the day off, but Bev was not having it. She was helping come Hell or high water. So, we took her up on her offer, and promised we would find someone to watch the kids on Wednesday if my parents were still sick.

As I went to bed that night, I couldn't help but feel something was off. It was just off. I didn't typically worry about my parents. It is just natural to see your parents as bullet proof, so I thought this was another one of those times. I was wrong, dead wrong!

I tossed and turned all night worrying about Wednesday. I mean sure, we had the next day covered, but 'what if' we were stuck again on Wednesday? There was no way in Hell I was asking a 77-year-old woman to watch a near four old, and a near one old for three straight days. I didn't sleep a wink that night, not one wink. Anxiety for a parent comes in many different forms.

It turned out I was right to be nervous because when I called my Dad the next day to check in on Mom, they weren't home, they were at the hospital. Mom had begun to bleed internally throughout that Monday night, and she was spitting up and pissing blood. This was no longer a cold, something was seriously wrong.

I told Dad to keep me posted, and I would check back in after work. Again, not that I was cold and callous, but Mom had been in and out of hospitals for various reasons her entire life. This was just one more time I thought. She had epilepsy amongst several other medical conditions that she battled throughout the years. This was far from her first hospital stay.

★★★

Most little girls grow up dreaming of marrying their prince charming and having children and living happily ever after. Sure, some dream of being movie stars, athletes, and music stars, but at the very root of it, they dream of being normal. To live a life full of dreams and happiness is the common goal. No one ever dreams of being sick, let alone developing an illness that can be crippling. For every school dance that maybe didn't go just right, or every boy who forgot to call, there was someone out there with even bigger problems and challenges. This is the story of that girl. One who only wanted to be normal and loved. Sadly, a crippling illness called epilepsy almost took that away from her forever.

Mom, Maria, was born August 15, 1956 at Marymount Hospital in Cleveland, Ohio. There was the assumption that the blessed mother Mary of Jesus would forever be a strong force in her life. Mom would be taught from a young age the importance of the Virgin Mother Mary from her Roman Catholic background. Mom was born into what would become a large family, and one never short on love. They were the typical Italian Catholic family.

Her parents, Joe and Rosemarie DeLuca, had met in high school and fell in love. In fact, Grandpa uttered the words, 'I'm going to marry that girl,' upon setting eyes on Grandma for the very first time. They went to school at John Adams High School and even after his family moved to Bay Village at the beginning of his senior year of high school, he kept dating Grandma and their love for one another grew. They got married soon after high school and Grandpa was drafted into the army during the Korean War, shortly after their wedding. It wasn't long after he left for war that their oldest child Josephine was born. It would be six months before he saw his first-born daughter for the first time. Grandpa would eventually return home from the military and the DeLuca family grew from there. Mom was the third born of eight children. Her older siblings, Josephine and Peter, came before Mom. My grandparents went on to have five more kids following Mom, brothers Joseph and Jimmy, along with sisters Rosemarie, Frances and Anna. It was a packed house with plenty of action, love and homemade food! Money was always tight because of the ten people living under one roof and the DeLucas being a one income family with Grandpa working as a postal worker, but love and fresh baked bread were always abundant. Mom and her siblings learned the value of hard work and sacrifice from an early age. Excellent values that they passed on to their own children.

Mom's life started a few hours later than maybe it should have. The doctor was late arriving, and despite Grandma being fully dilated, the nurse urged her to hold the baby in. She was ready to come into the world, but the world was not yet ready for her. The preventing of her life arriving was the start of lifelong issues she would be forced to endure. By the time it was time for Mom to arrive, the doctor needed to use forceps to get her out which caused brain damage. This is not common, but in her case, it happened and it would be the beginning of major concern. It caused brain tissue to be scarred. She was fighting an uphill battle minutes after being born.

External head trauma from forceps or vacuum extractors can lead to injuries such as hematomas (brain bleeds), skull fractures, hydrocephalus (build-up of fluid in the brain) and other potentially serious injuries that can affect the brain and cause different types of seizures. The medical field recently did a study on this and came back with some very alarming results. A total of 381 children born with forceps delivery and 372 with normal delivery were followed up for four to seven years. More children in the forceps group developed seizures than in the normal group, i.e. 22:10. This was statistically significant ($p < 0.05$). There was no neurological deficit in any child who had seizures. Both partial and generalized seizures were seen, but partial seizures were more frequent.

As Mom grew up very early on, she had a few seizures as an infant. Not many, but when they did happen the doctors referred to them as 'febrile seizures.' They most commonly occur in children between the ages of 6 months and 5 years. Seizures occur when there is a sudden, uncontrolled electrical disturbance in the brain. While some people are diagnosed with idiopathic (unpreventable) epilepsy, many other people experience seizures due to injury. Trauma to the head during, or shortly after birth, can definitely cause seizures. The head and brain are so delicate in the first weeks of life, it is important that any suspected illness or injury is recognized, diagnosed, and treated immediately.

This was believed to be the case with Mom. It was common. The doctors and others never thought to look further into it. A febrile seizure is associated with a high body temperature but without any serious underlying health issue. The reason why it wasn't looked into right away was because most seizures are less than five minutes in duration and the child is completely back to normal within sixty minutes of the event. Long term outcomes are generally good with little risk of neurological problems or epilepsy.

Simple febrile seizures do not tend to recur frequently and do not make the development of adult epilepsy significantly more likely compared with the general public. Only about 1% of infants who suffer from frequent febrile seizures go on to develop severe epilepsy as adults, sadly for Mom, she fell into that 1%. Seizures can be either temporary, or may be recurring, which is diagnosed as the disease epilepsy. Epilepsy is among the oldest and most common neurological disorders diagnosed worldwide. It is estimated that 30 percent of individuals living with epilepsy are children. Unfortunately, most people are unaware of just how seizures or epilepsy affects sufferers and their families.

Looking more in depth, the range of severity and symptoms associated with seizures is quite broad. Depending on what part of the brain was injured, and to what extent, often determines what symptoms are present. For Mom, the warning signs of epilepsy would go past febrile seizures as she grew past her toddler years and became a little girl. She would begin to wake up in the middle of the night with full body muscle spasms in her arms and legs. This is more commonly known as a 'charley horse' and can become quite painful. But these weren't just charley horses, they were much worse. She would wake up in the middle of the night with intense pain and screaming in agony, waking up the entire packed house. Grandma would run in and rub her legs down, work out the cramps and do whatever she could to comfort her daughter until she was able to lay back down and fall asleep.

When telling the doctors about her muscle spasms, their solution was to increase potassium in her diet, so Mom would start each day out with an orange and banana. It didn't help and the daily pain continued to intensify. Life was different for Mom growing up for obvious reasons and she didn't know why early on. She just knew that she was different then her older sister Josephine, and teachers didn't hesitate to remind her. As the third child of eight, she was always asked by the teachers why she did things so differently than her older siblings, Josephine and Peter. She was trying to find her way, and not knowing the full extent of her issues just yet, life was very hard.

Mom didn't realize she had epilepsy yet, but she knew something was different and wrong growing up. The other kids realized something was wrong as well as she had several classmates in kindergarten through sixth grade that would tease and pick on her. The teachers were uneducated at the time about the illness. They didn't know how to recognize signs of it and treated her like an outcast instead of offering her help. In fact, teachers could actually be the biggest bullies back then. Instead of understanding, the teacher would just stand there and yell at her to stop until the horrible ordeal was over. Her classmates, at first in shock, would eventually start getting used to it and begin to laugh at Mom during the seizures. This could happen up to ten times in a day when you factor in all the bells ringing throughout the day and all the time a teacher would flick a light switch on and off. It got so bad early on that every time a loud or sharp sound would go off, Mom would fall into that deep dark place of agony by herself. It ravaged her body so badly that most times the seizures would cause her to pee her pants, and she would have to wear soiled clothes for the remainder of the day until she returned home from school.

So, scared of ever having a full bladder, Mom would skip drinking anything at lunch or at any time throughout the school day. She was so desperate to hide things that she would purposely sit in the mud, or a puddle in the schoolyard to cover up an accident that had just occurred in her pants. She resorted to wearing several layers of underwear on most school days, hoping that it would soak up her urine before others could see it. It didn't always work, most times the urine would still soak through her clothes which only led to more name calling and harassment from her classmates.

The seven years between kindergarten and sixth grade were the worst of her life. At the time, the seizures were small but without any-one knowing what was wrong with her, she became awkward, scared and alone. She didn't feel accepted and was scared every single day when she woke up.

★★★

Despite all the sadness in her life, Mom was starting to develop a hidden talent for drawing and artwork that no one saw yet. When Mom had a project that consisted of any form of artwork for her other classes such as history or science, she would turn in incredible work. However, the teachers would fail her because they did not believe it was her doing the work. They insisted it was her brother, Peter or her father. The teachers refused to believe the beautiful work was coming from her. Mom would offer to prove it by drawing something right there on the spot, but the teachers wouldn't even allow that. It wasn't until many years later when she had children that her aspiration to draw was fulfilled as she was given the chance to draw for her two sons.

As Mom continued to grow up, things began to increase in difficulty at a different level. She started 'womanhood' early, getting her first period at the age of 11-years-old. Ironically enough at the same time, her mother was in the hospital getting a hysterectomy as she had just had her eighth child and was done having babies. My Mom's menstrual cycle beginning caused a new type of seizure to begin. This new seizure was referred to as a 'temporal lobe seizure.'

Temporal lobe epilepsy is a chronic neurological condition characterized by recurrent, unprovoked epileptic seizures which originate in the temporal lobe of the brain. The seizures involve sensory changes or a memory disturbance. The most common cause is mesial temporal sclerosis (deep scarring in the temporal lobe). Temporal lobe epilepsy (TLE) is the single most common form of a partial seizure. The causes of TLE include mesial temporal sclerosis, traumatic brain injury, brain infections, such as encephalitis and meningitis, hypoxic brain injury, stroke, cerebral tumors, and genetic syndromes.

It is important to note and understand that 'TLE is not the result of mental health disorders or fragility of the personality.' It has nothing to do with how someone lives their life; how their personality is or anything they do. The person with TLE is stuck with it, and it could happen to anyone. It *shouldn't* make them an outcast. Anyone who sees it that way is mis-informed and closed minded. People can't help it that they have seizures and for others to laugh at them for it is sick and inexcusable.

Mom did have some hope as she entered sixth-grade. It was junior high and kids from other grade Clara schools would be joining her at West Drop Junior High. These were kids who didn't know her and may not judge her, meaning she *actually* had a chance to make a friend, if not several. Helping matters for Mom as she reached junior high was the fact that older brother Peter was very popular because of his great artistic ability, a three-sport star athlete and good looks. Peter had made the DeLuca name proud. Another reason why he was so loved was because of his very kind heart.

Those plans of sudden popularity were dashed however with the signs of epilepsy still not detected and without her teachers being able to understand how to treat her. Mom was moved to the special classes for troubled kids. She was mixed in with students who were very bad, and others who were labelled slow, handicapped and almost a lost cause. Mom was neither slow nor stupid, but she was unfairly labelled because of a condition she couldn't control. All of those labelled were located in the same hallway and the other students would refer to it as the 'dummy hall.'

It was during this stretch however that Mom finally had a breakthrough. She had eighth period, English, taught by Mr. Lawrence Frye. He would change her life as he not only taught her how to read properly, but also was the first person to truly recognize that something may be wrong beyond her control. He saw something in Mom's face during a seizure that until then had gone unrecognized. Mr. Frye had a family member with epilepsy and knew exactly what was going on with Mom. He was the first teacher that didn't yell at Mom for being bad; he understood what torture she was being forced to endure. He was very understanding and was the first person who finally alerted her parents to what was going on and the serious problem she had. This was only two weeks into her sixth-grade school year and Mom would now have to miss many days of school because her parents were unable to get her in with brain specialist doctors to begin treatment.

The doctors began to treat Mom by asking many different questions to find out exactly how bad it was. She would enter Fairview Hospital to begin a series of tests. One of which was a very painful and scary procedure called a spinal tap. A spinal tap is used to collect cerebrospinal fluid to confirm or exclude conditions such as meningitis and subarachnoid hemorrhage and it may be used in diagnosis of other conditions. The patient is usually placed in a left lateral position with their neck bent in full flexion and knees bent in full flexion up to their chest, approximating a fetal position as much as possible. The area around the lower back is prepared using aseptic technique. Once the appropriate location is palpated, local anesthetic is infiltrated under the skin and then injected along the intended path of the spinal needle. A spinal needle is inserted between the lumbar vertebrae L3/L4, L4/L5.

The patient would often be asked to lie on their back for at least six hours and be monitored for signs of neurological problems. Patient anxiety during the procedure can lead to increased cerebrospinal fluid (CSF) pressure. Especially, if the person holds their breath, tenses their muscles or flexes their knees too tightly against their chest. Side effects during the procedure are serious as well. Some side effects include spinal or epidural bleeding, adhesive arachnoiditis and trauma to the spinal cord or spinal nerve roots resulting in weakness or loss of sensation, or even paraplegia. A spinal tap can also result in perforation of abnormal dural arterio-venous malformations, resulting in catastrophic epidural hemorrhage. Removal of cerebrospinal fluid resulting in reduced fluid pressure has been shown to correlate with greater reduction of cerebral blood flow among patients with Alzheimer's disease.

Can you imagine being 14 or 15 years old, and having to endure this? While most girls at that age are worried about a zit, or not fitting into skinny jeans, Mom had to endure this type of torture. This was only the beginning.

The doctors sat Mom in a high chair with the back open and strapped her arms and legs down so tight she couldn't move them at all. Her head was placed in a helmet-like contraption and she couldn't move it either. This is done so the person can't squirm or mess up the placement of the giant needle going into the patient's back. The specialists proceeded to put needles into her back that went straight through to the vertebrae in her spine, draining fluid from it. They then put in syringes filled with dye which they proceeded to also inject into her back. They even told her it was okay to scream because they knew it would be extremely painful.

After the spinal tap procedure was done the next test consisted of Mom being curled into a little ball and carted into the x-ray room for another series of x-rays. After that, she was wheeled back into the room for a short period of rest. Mom was stubborn; she didn't want to give into the pain and didn't want anyone knowing how bad it felt. Instead of screaming, she asked for a wash cloth and bit down on it as hard as she could to avoid screaming. Shortly after the testing was done, she was diagnosed with epilepsy. She had never heard of it, but Grandpa did as his cousin suffered from it.

Back then this was such a dark cloud that most people didn't share that they had it, and many families would try to ignore it. The DeLuca family was very different; they loved Mom and began to adjust life for her condition. Mom's parents were very loving to their whole family, and didn't treat her differently. They shared her story with other families to spread the message and look for a cure. Mom was blessed to be a part of the DeLuca family that sat 10 to a dinner table every night. Grandpa worked his tail off, taking care of all of them on a postal worker's salary. The family knew of hard times but also knew how to love one another. Despite the condition, her parents did not keep her from doing things she wanted to do. They let her help with chores around the house, with eight kids, there was never a shortage of beds to be made or rooms to be cleaned. Grandma didn't hesitate to teach her how to cook, something Mom would love to do. They allowed Mom to run, jump, ride a bike, do all the things kids do. They didn't want to keep her in a bubble despite how serious things were. They allowed her to have a childhood under caution, but none the less, a childhood!

My Grandparents did their best to keep things positive for Mom because when they sat down with the doctor, it was nothing but bad news. While he never took the time to explain what epilepsy was, he didn't hesitate to tell the DeLucas all the things Mom would never be able to do or achieve in life. It wasn't a short list. The doctor said:

1. Her family would grow to be ashamed of her and more than likely put her in a mental hospital.
2. She would never be able to operate a vehicle and never obtain a driver's license.
3. Sled riding was out; bike riding was out, any form of fun for a child was out. Everything from cheerleading to jumping rope was out.

4. And explained how she would never have a boyfriend, get married and she could forget about having children. Because no man would ever want to be with her, and if for some reason she found a man, giving birth could and would kill her.

Mom was young, naive, and taught to respect her elders. She was under the impression that if a teacher or doctor said it, then it would have to be correct. However, she was also stubborn, strong willed and wouldn't allow anyone anywhere to tell her she couldn't follow her dreams. She made a promise to herself that one day she would drive a car and get married. She was too young to realize how babies were made, but by golly, she would figure that out too. No one on planet Earth was going to tell her she wouldn't one day become a mommy. For the next decade, Mom would see this doctor and hear about all the things she would never accomplish, and for the next several decades Mom did everything she could to prove him wrong!

These checkups would continue every three months and most times, Mom would be in the cold waiting room, wearing nothing but a thin paper gown waiting hours for this man to come in and examine her. He would never explain anything, or even give coping techniques; he would simply ask how many seizures she had had since her last visit and proceed with his examination. He wasn't looking for a solution as much as he was just monitoring it. It was very uncomfortable for Mom because the examination process required her to walk back and forth in front of him wearing a gown that did not close in the back. The examination also called for him to touch her in all of her nerve endings, including the ones in private areas. Making things even more uncomfortable for the young woman was that he would have her bend over and touch her toes, while he probed areas that had nerve endings. A humiliating examination for anyone to have to endure, let alone a young scared girl.

The seizures would get worse as the years passed. Mom was lucky, however, that she had the same teachers all through junior high school. She loved them because they understood her and knew how to handle her. They knew how she felt and what she was going through. Junior high only lasts three years and eventually she would have to graduate and start high school at John Marshall. It was a school whose reputation would become synched with the DeLuca name in the sixties and seventies because of the outstanding athletic performances of her brothers Peter, Joey and Jim. Peter would finish second in the entire state of Ohio in 1973, in wrestling. He was also a three-sport letterman and captain in football and baseball as well. Peter could do it all.

Yet despite strong family presence in the school, Mom was still afraid because it meant new classmates, new teachers and new challenges. Sadly, for Mom, her fears became justified as the seizures became worse, much worse as they developed into the dreaded 'grand mal' seizure. This is a form of epilepsy characterized by tonic-clonic seizures involving two phases. The tonic phase in which the body becomes rigid, and clonic phase in which there is uncontrolled jerking. Tonic-clonic seizures may or may not be preceded by an aura, and are often followed by headache, confusion, and sleep. They may last for mere seconds, or continue for several minutes. In more common terms, they are large and dramatic, and there is no way to ignore them or hide them. It stops your entire day, and sometimes puts a person out of commission for several days.

The bullying got worse in high school because of the dramatic seizures. Mom would describe them as feeling like her brain was on fire and her whole body was being electrocuted. She would end up biting her tongue during the seizures and her eyes would roll back in her head. Her entire body would fall to the floor and go into a large uncontrollable spasm.

It is one of the most horrible sights anyone can ever have to witness. Her arms, legs and head would bang into whatever was near them. She would also lose control of her full bladder. The worst part was that while all of this was going on, she was aware of what was going on and couldn't do anything to stop it. Students having to witness this would scream in fear at the sight. Sadly, the sounds of fear from the classmates would also be accompanied by the sounds of laughter. The students would stand around calling her names as she was flopping on the floor in need of someone to hold her down so she wouldn't get hurt.

Mom would often black out, waking up minutes and sometimes hours later in the nurses' office. She would change her clothes into dry ones, then have to go right back to class. The other students would snicker at her as she walked to her next class. She would pray that the bells would not set off another attack as she walked. The school would eventually realise that they needed to adapt to the situation at hand and figure out a safe area of the school they could bring Mom to before each class was over and the bell rang. That way, in the case of a seizure, there would be people there ready to help her. Sometimes it worked, sometimes it didn't.

One person who stood by Mom's side in school was close friend, Patty Lynch. Patty helped Mom when she was down and stuck up for her when others would put her down. Patty even threw Mom a surprise 16th birthday party. It was an act of kindness that Mom has never forgotten.

Against doctor's orders, Mom tried out for the JV cheerleading squad at John Marshall. She knew the dangers at hand and that the doctor told her she would never make an organised team, but she was never one not to try something she truly believed she could do. Her doctor wouldn't even allow her to take gym class. Mom was determined to prove him wrong and begin fulfilling dreams. The day of tryouts came and she nailed her entire routine during tryouts. She did everything she had to do to make the team and performed well. Just as she was wrapping up her routine during the tryout, she went for a cartwheel. During this process the school bell rang and she went into a seizure mid cartwheel. She was lucky enough to be on a padded mat and to come out of the seizure quickly, but still scared and embarrassed at what happened she ran out of the gym, and ran the entire four-mile trip home in her wet gym clothes.

Later that night Mom received a call that was step one in proving the doctors wrong, and also her first step towards achieving multiple dreams in her life. She had made the team! Mom was not even close to being done with breaking down barriers yet. Being a part of a large family on one income meant that having a part time job in high school was a must. Once again, the doctor had told her active employment was not an option, and that her being a productive member of society was next to impossible. Mom was determined to get that part time job and help her family anyway she could.

In the summer following her tenth-grade year of high school she started working for Riverside Nursing Home as a nurse's aid. She loved the job even as hard as the physical labor was. There was no bell ringing every hour and the one phone they had was at a front desk with a very soft buzz, not even a ring to it. During the week she would work as an aid after school and on Sundays they had her in the kitchen cooking. It was a small nursing home with only 38 patients, but Mom relished the chance to help others. Some of the patients really didn't need to be there; they just had nowhere else to go. Some would come in for rehab but never leave as their family left them there to die. This did not matter to Mom because she loved and cared for all of the patients. It soon became a family affair as her older sister Josephine became a nurse there as she was in nursing school at the time. Her brothers Peter and Joey were working there part-time as janitors and her sister Rose was washing dishes.

When Mom wasn't working or cheering, she still wanted to pursue her love of art. As she sat with the school counsellors, she pleaded with them to let her take art classes. The school refused to bend on their rules and continued to tell her that she couldn't take art classes because she wasn't smart enough. The other fear was that with all the sharp objects in an art class someone could get seriously hurt if she began to seizure. Instead of art class, they did allow her to take cooking class. Which made little to no sense because despite her love of cooking, it was odd that the school would encourage her to be around hot boiling pans, sharp knives and hot ovens. It made little to no sense, but she made the most of it.

★★★

All of that was running through my mind as I left work that Tuesday afternoon. Mom had been through so many dark tunnels in her life, and always came out ahead. Why would a bad chest cold be any different? I mean sure, the pissing blood thing had me concerned, but I just refused to believe we had anything too serious to worry about. Call it ignorance, call it blind faith, I wasn't having it any different.

Two seconds after walking into her hospital room on Tuesday night April 18th, refusing to have fear turned into a stark contrast with reality. Mom wasn't just sick. She was on her way to fighting the greatest battle of her life, and we were just getting started.

CHAPTER THREE

'Face reality as it is, not as it was or as you wish it to be.' – Jack Welch

This is serious?

As I heard my Dad talking with the doctor on Tuesday night, I quickly realized "who was going to watch the girls" was the least of my worries. Suddenly, we were up against something bigger than us. I still had hope that this was "just pneumonia" and my Mom would get better quickly. However, all signs were starting to point towards one hell of a battle none of us saw coming.

The doctor explained that if Mom didn't show signs of improvement, they might have to move her from a normal room into the ICU. Yeah right, I thought, this is Maria McKee you're talking about. She will be outside smoking a Newport 100 before this guy's head hits the pillow tonight. But, again, anytime a doctor says something, you have to realize he is basing it off statistics and possible worst case scenarios.

So, I gave my Mom a kiss, a hug and told her, 'okay Mom, enough days off, get your stuff together already.' Clearly joking. We had that kind of relationship, always pushing each other to be better. She had pushed me since I was a little kid to always do and be my best. She was my toughest critic but also my biggest supporter. We also stuck up for each other tooth and nail, even when we knew the other one might be wrong. It was what family did.

★★★

Case in point, there was a time in the summer of 1995 that my best friend, Dave Murphy, slept over. We kept prank calling this random guy all night long. It was out of character for Dave and I, but for some reason that night we felt like being idiots. Sure enough, the very next morning at about 6 a.m., the guy called our house pissed off. The rocket scientists that Dave and I were, never factored in the beauty of caller

ID. The phone rings and we could hear through the wall Dad say, "who the hell is calling this early in the morning?" From there we proceed to overhear my Mom pick up the phone and exchange in an epic argument with this poor guy for at least five minutes about how her son and his angel of a friend would never do such a thing. Again, it was very much out of character for Dave and I, but even if it was, she went into instant mother mode. After what seemed like an eternity, she finally hangs up on him. About five seconds of silence go by when we can hear Dad say, "You know he probably did it, right?" Followed by Mom quickly agreeing and saying, "Yeah, I know." Followed by the prompt lighting of a Newport 100. If there was anything Mom loved, it was cooking for others, followed closely by a good verbal joust.

And yes, for those wondering, she did beat my butt for prank calling the guy about two minutes after Dave left to go home later that morning. Back then, it was normal to discipline that way, there was no "counting to ten" in the McKee home. It was a reason why *I* seldom ever got in trouble in or out of school. I had my moments like any kid, but knowing that my parents were serious, kept me on the straight and narrow. Don't get me wrong, my parents always made sure I kept on the straight and narrow. Twelve years of school with never once getting in trouble proved that. But my Mom and I weren't strangers to covering for each other when we had to. Another classic was the summer of '93 when my Mom got pegged for driving 44mph in a 25mph school zone with me in the car. It was a Sunday, so no school, but the police officer didn't get care. Mom begged me not to tell Dad, so I agreed. I don't think my Dad would have even cared as it was an honest mistake, but she was embarrassed so I never said anything.

Well, that isn't entirely true I guess, as I didn't hesitate to mention the number, '44' in her presence over the next few weeks. If I wanted extra anything, it was '44.' *How about a special trip to Toy's R Us? No, well that's okay Mom because I just counted my action figures and I have exactly '44' Hulk Hogans. Oh, what is that you say?* On the way to Toy's R Us we went.

We never had a lot of money growing up. Almost never did we get anything from Dairy Queen, other than small vanilla ice cream cones the three or four times a year we actually went there. My brother Don and I didn't care. We weren't spoiled kids and we were just happy to have parents who loved us and were home every night. Well, after I mentioned to my Mom that week that Dairy Queen had exactly '44' ice cream combinations on their menu, sure enough I got a blizzard that trip. The fun of blackmail only lasted a few weeks until my Dad got the insurance paperwork in the mail notifying him of the price increase because of the added points to their policy. The secret was out of the bag, but it was fun while it lasted. As I expected, my Dad understood.

The funny thing was that despite her horrible driving, she was actually in the process of doing something incredible that week with Don. They were set to travel to Colorado with their church group to see Pope John Paul II. It was a special trip that meant a lot to the both of them. That was my Mom, her heart and love for all things Mary and Jesus could never be questioned.

The fun of '44' wasn't the only time we had some hijinks on the roadways together. When I was really little, about five or six years old, we went go-karting. My brother sat with Dad and I sat with Mom. They were larger cars that required a parent with anyone under ten. Well, I wasn't going to let the thrill and power of being behind the wheel for the first time go without extreme calamity. The second I felt the roar of the engine and the power inside me flair up at the feeling of a gas pedal, it was all over! Things started off innocently enough as Mom did the bulk of the driving the first couple of laps. It was then that I channeled my inner Mario Andretti and took control of the wheel and the gas. At five years old I could barely see over the wheel, but that wasn't stopping me. I proceeded to floor it with full steam. The problem was I didn't account for the sharp turn ahead and we went off roading.

Most go-kart tracks are built so you slam against the protective wall if you try going

AWOL, this one was not. Instead, this track was surrounded by huge bales of hay. They didn't stand a chance as we busted through them like the Kool Aid Man slamming through a wall. You would think the guy running the track would have had some mercy on us, but he didn't. Like Spence from the pool, Mom and I were banned from the race-track forever that day.

In what could only be described as pure irony, new owners would buy that Go-Kart company about 30 years later. They became one of my first sponsors when I started my own media company, KEE On Sports Media Group. Clearly, they didn't know about my horrible history at the track.

Perhaps my favorite Mom high jinks moment, and trust me when I tell you there were plenty of them, had to be when I visited Dave Murphy at Xavier College in the Spring of 2004. In fact, this story is so memorable that I often still think about it and laugh to this day. It was a sunny Friday afternoon as I packed my bag and got ready to visit Dave for a fun filled weekend at Xavier University in Cincinnati. He was a senior there and I had already made plenty of trips to go visit him; each time brought on its own stories. This time however, I decided to have a little fun before I left. I was still living at home at the time, and both my parents were at work. As I went to turn my alarm clock off so it wouldn't buzz the next morning when I wouldn't be home, it hit me like a thunder bolt as to what needed to be done. Not only did I not turn it off, I set the alarm to go off at 3:30 a.m. the next morning. Thus, Mom or Dad would hear it and have to get out of bed pissed off to turn it off. I then went into my parents' room with the knowledge they never set their alarms on the weekend, and proceeded to set my Mom's to go off at 3:45 a.m. and then my Dad's to go off at 4:00 a.m.

You would think that would be enough, three alarms within 30 minutes of each other, but I knew if I was going to pull this off in epic fashion, I had to go for the gold. Don had moved out two years prior, but they never really used his room for anything, or even switched it. I went ahead and took the alarm clock that was in his room, which was still in the closet, and proceeded to put batteries in it, and set it under my parents' bed to go off at 4:15 a.m. I knew what I was doing was wrong, and I knew the backlash would be fierce, but it still didn't stop me from swinging by CVS five minutes later and buying one last alarm clock. Yet another that could be powered by battery, and one that I would return home briefly to place directly in my Dad's underwear drawer to go off at 4:30 a.m.

I forgot all about it about five minutes after I hit I-71 South on my way down to the Queen City. It wasn't until about 7 a.m. the next morning after being out partying all night that I remembered what I did. The reason for my sudden recall was my phone ringing with my Mom on the other end. The phone call lasted all of five seconds and consisted of only her talking after I said, "hello." My Mom managed to get out, "don't come home." Until I hung up in one of those "oh shit" moments, when it finally came to me what I had done.

By the time I got home Sunday afternoon, the heat on me had blown over and all was forgiven. I was thrown off for a second however when the newspaper was turned to the apartment listing and set strategically on my bed when I returned. All in good fun and I'm pretty sure my daughters will get me every bit as bad one day. This was just the kind of relationship Mom and I had over the years. We were tough on each other and argued like cats and dogs, but we also cared about each other like only a mother and son can. I knew no matter how bad I screwed something up, she'd be there for me. It was the same when I did something great, no one would be prouder.

***

As Dad walked with me to the parking garage to get my car, I could sense he was a little unnerved this time around. Something just seemed like there was more to this whole thing that we didn't know just yet. We'd both quickly find out just how bad it was very soon.

Upon returning home, I had a missed call from Carrie Pell. Now Carrie was as close to an angel on Earth as there ever was one over the years. She worked with Emily's Dad at FedEx but also had a side business as a photographer. As one with many jobs myself, I could respect the crap out of anyone working a full-time job, and then chasing their dream full time on the side.

Carrie was just this incredible person inside and out. She was absolutely beautiful. In her late 50s she looked as though she could be in her 30s with no problems at all. She also had this smile that could light up a room two seconds after walking in. She had a heart of gold, a soul of kindness and was one of the most genuine human beings I have ever met in my life. I could close my eyes right now and still hear her voice and remember her smile. She was the photographer for my wedding, which she did at cost. She was that kind and so is her husband, Lou. Carrie tragically and suddenly passed away in December of 2017 from a sudden bout of leukemia. She left behind children, grandchildren and a loving husband in Lou. It sucks having to write this part because the world needs more people like Carrie Pell. I think about her and miss her a lot.

The reason Carrie Pell was calling was to check in on my Mom. I hadn't put anything on Facebook or social media of any kind yet, and at that time didn't think it was needed. However, my father-in-law mentioned that my Mom was in the hospital to Carrie at work so she reached out on her own. Her second question after checking in on my Mom was, "who is watching the kids?" After I told her that Emily or I were going to have to miss work, she said, "absolutely not" and volunteered to use her one day off a week to help. She wasn't going to take no for an answer either. She was that damn good a person. I can never put it into words, or even try to put it into words just how special she was to my life.

With Carrie set to be there in the morning, it helped me sleep a little bit, that and the calmness of knowing Mom was tough and things would be back to normal by the weekend. Or at least I kept telling myself that. Things always seemed to get better by the weekend. Or maybe it just seemed that way at times. After thanking Carrie, the next morning, I was on my 55-minute drive to work and focused on the day ahead. I used part of my lunch break to call Dad and check in. He didn't answer. That was odd as he usually would answer on the first or second ring. I did a quick Google search and found the phone number for Fairview Hospital and called them directly.

At first, the receptionist told me that Mom was no longer in her room and must have checked out. I was relieved to hear that and was about to hang up when the nurse said, "Oh wait, I found her, she is in ICU, would you like to be connected with a nurse?" My emotions went from ecstatic to scared within seconds, not the first time that would be happening that week. The nurse and then later my Dad would both explain that Mom had worsened throughout the night and they transported her to the intensive care unit (ICU) section of the hospital. She was struggling to breathe even with help, and that made the move mandatory as she was no longer in a stable condition, but rather a critical one.

For those of you reading this, unfamiliar with the 'ICU,' it is the section of the hospital used to provide intensive care for critically ill patients. It is the last stop before either getting better or passing away. With this knowledge in my mind, I headed straight to the hospital from work after punching out at the end of the day. I did my best to keep my mind on work. The best I could following the lunch phone call; the news was unsettling to say the least. Between each call, I would say a mini prayer and try to rationalize in my head what was going on.

The drive from work to the hospital turned out to be nothing less than stressful. I'll never forget how hard it was raining that day. It was pouring to the point where some cars had to pull off the road on the highway until it calmed down. I was unfazed by the storm as it seemed as though time was standing still at moments on that drive. The only positive thing about the rain was that it was strong enough to cancel

Maggie's soccer practice that day. I say that was a good thing simply because it allowed me to get to the hospital quicker. I made a vow to Emily early into my writing career that I would never miss anything with my children, no matter the situation. It was bad enough I had to miss a few hours on Easter a few days prior, I wasn't about to miss soccer practice too.

I just kept thinking that Mom would get better and all of this was overkill. I thought that at least until I arrived at the ICU, but Mom could barely catch her breath. I could sense immediately that things were not good and much worse than we all thought it would be. I called Emily and let her know that I wouldn't be home for many hours that night. She had gone straight home to relieve Carrie. I then called Don, my only sibling, and let him know that he may want to come in from North Carolina if things didn't start improving.

Don and his family had lived in Apex North Carolina since 2009. It was always nice when he would visit, especially after him and his wife, Abbie, adopted my nephew, Matthew. Times spent with Matt on visits are always some of the best. In a way, it is my way to know what it feels like to have a son and a little brother all at once. Matt was also a great cousin to my girls and it was impossible not to have fun with Matt around.

I told Don that it wasn't looking good and that I would know by tomorrow if he was going to need to come in. I then called Carrie and thanked her again for watching the girls. Little did I know that would be the final time I ever heard her voice. My skin gets goosebumps and an icy chill as I even type that. I'll say it again, she was an angel on Earth, and is now an angel in Heaven.

I stuck around the hospital until about 11 p.m. that night and sat with my cousins, Tony, Gena and Frances as they all came to visit. I could tell Dad was starting to get worried too, but this was far from the first time in his relationship with Mom that her health was far from good. In fact, he had stuck by her since day one. Mom had met Dad through her friend, who had set Mom up on a date for her prom. Until then, no guy would show even the smallest bit of attraction to my Mom because of the epilepsy she suffered from. As we know, kids could be very cruel.

***

In her first three plus years of high school, and all the preceding years before it, Mom never had a boyfriend. Guys didn't date girls like her: girls who were unfairly labelled retarded. The boys were pleasant to her in groups, but didn't want to be alone with her in case she might seizure. Some guys would ask her out thinking that she would be so desperate for male attention that she would instantly have sex with them. They quickly discovered she was not that kind of girl and moved on. No matter where she was, if she was put into that type of situation with a guy, she would instantly leave and walk away no matter how far from home. It was hard for Mom to trust or feel comfortable around anyone. It was a different time back then, people were every bit as cruel to others, but they didn't have social media to hide behind. It was around this time that some of the boys in school would begin a cruel joke that no person anywhere should have to suffer through, let alone a young woman with epilepsy. A random senior in high school would ask Mom out, take her to a nice restaurant and then skip out on the bill and leave her to pay it and walk home.

That would all change when she met Dad. He was the star wrestler at rival high school West Tech and had graduated a few years prior. Dad had come from a broken home and did not have the best of reputations. Dad fell in love with Mom instantly, but because of how many times she had been hurt in the past, Mom was unwilling to even entertain the thought of speaking with him. On March 28, 1974 Dad called the DeLuca house and asked to speak with Mom. This time, unlike the others she decided to take the call. He told her he wanted to take her to prom. Mom was nervous and told him that he would have to meet Grandpa first. She explained to him that if her parents approved of him, she would go to prom with him. He showed up at the house about six o'clock, and didn't leave until well after midnight. He spent almost the entire night talking with Grandpa about high school wrestling. Dad was a superstar at West Tech and Uncle Peter was at John Marshall, so they had a lot of mutual interests to speak about.

On May 3, 1974, Dad once again showed up on the DeLuca front steps, this time to bring Mom to church and then meet his Mom. It was evening mass that night and didn't start until 6 p.m., but he was at the DeLuca home at 4 p.m. All of her younger brothers and sisters were playing with him, joking and having fun for the entire two hours before church. As Mom was getting ready, she kept peeking her head out the door and was happy to see how well her family took to him. She entered the room wearing a beautiful church dress. Dad's face was stunned and happy as he proclaimed, he had never seen a girl so beautiful in a dress. The few weeks of dating him consisted of him coming over to talk with her father about sports and also play around with all of her brothers and sisters. It was clear, Dad had found a family that he loved being around. They took a lot of walks together and did plenty of talking, getting to know each other on a much deeper level. The closer they grew together the greater the fear Mom had of having a seizure in front of him became. At first, she could hide the small ones, but she knew she wouldn't be able to hide the big ones. She didn't realize he already knew about her illness and it didn't bug him. She was scared that when he found out he would run away from her like so many others did in the past.

Prom weekend finally arrived and Mom was never more nervous than she was that day. She had long hair past her shoulders that she played with all day to make sure it was perfect for the big dance. She picked out just the right dress, and it was beautiful. She had gone to the store with her oldest sister Josephine and spent hours until finding just the right one. Dad showed up early, as usual, 4 p.m. to be exact. All of her siblings were there to keep him entertained while he waited for her. She had been having so many small seizures that day that she didn't get in the dress until the very last moment because she didn't want to risk ruining it.

Josephine fixed her hair, zipped up her dress and told her she looked beautiful. She told her she looked like a princess with tears rolling from her eyes. Shortly after that Grandma came in and echoed those same sentiments.

As fate would have it, the second Grandma and Josephine walked Mom to the living room so Dad could see her for the first time all dressed up beautiful, the damn phone rang and set off a small seizure for her. Josephine and Grandma quickly hurried Mom into the bathroom and helped her get cleaned up. They put extra padding in her dress and tried everything again. This time she walked out and Dad was standing there with the biggest smile on his face. He was holding a full bouquet of flowers and didn't hesitate to let her know how beautiful she looked to him.

Now, almost exactly 40 plus years later to the date, Dad wasn't worried about taking Mom to the prom, his main focus was not having to take her to the morgue. Things were starting to look bad, and it appeared that they would get worse before getting better, if they ever did. It was during that long visit that the decision was made, if Mom's breathing continued to worsen, they would put her on the ventilator to keep her breathing. The easiest way I can describe what that does is this. Picture a giant tube jammed down your throat so it does all the breathing for you. Most times, the patient is sedated into a comatose state, so they won't pull the tube out, and allow it to work. Once you're on the vent, few come off so most times it is an absolute death sentence. It becomes a ticking time bomb in a way because you can only stay on that ventilator for 14 days before a decision is made to pull you off of it and let you die. Or perform a tracheotomy.

What is a tracheotomy you may ask? The simplest explanation I can give is that they cut a hole in your neck or throat area and jam a tube in there to help you breathe. This occurs when you can no longer stay on the vent past 14 days because of the risk of an infection. For those of you who prefer the exact detailed, less gruesome description, here it is. A tracheotomy is a surgical procedure which consists of making an incision (cut) on the anterior aspect (front) of the neck and opening a direct airway through an incision in the trachea (windpipe). The resulting stoma (hole) can serve independently as an airway or as a site for a tracheal tube or tracheostomy tube to be inserted. This tube allows a person to breathe without the use of the nose or mouth.

★★★

As I drove home, I thought about the last words I left my Mom with that night before leaving, "get plenty of rest if they put you out because you're not dying on my watch." By put out, I meant going on the vent.

The crazy thing about all of this was that she wouldn't even be the first family member of ours to go on the vent. Back in 2009, Don obtained a virus known as "swine flu." Basically, it was like stomach flu, but about 100 times worse and killing people. It was more or less brand new to the public at that time and doctors were certainly challenged by it.

In November of 2009, when Don got it, it was still on the rise and seen as deadly. Don had gone into the hospital on a Tuesday night, and by the very next morning, he was on a vent struggling to live as the infection spread all over his body. Making things even worse was that it was Thanksgiving week and it was damn near impossible to jump on a plane and get there.

My parents managed to fly out Tuesday night and I got there first thing Wednesday morning. I'll never forget the airport that day. It was "nuts" as they say. The day before Thanksgiving is the busiest travel day of the year. To say the airport was packed would be a great understatement. It was insane! My eyes were bloodshot from lack of sleep and crying as I waited to board the plane. It was then that a fellow passenger offered me weed. Not sure how he thought we'd get away with it, but he was talking to the wrong guy on the wrong day.

I hate drugs, all drugs of any kind, no excuses. I especially hate weed. Yet again, an opinion that I thought anyone would share, but I sadly found out in my life that I'm in the minority on that one as well.

The way people causally smoke it pisses me off. I've never once, in my 38 years on this Earth ever heard a single person say, "yeah, my life really took off after I started smoking pot." I'm also pretty damn sure I've never heard an athlete say, "I owe my achievements to a lifetime of smoking the doobie." I mention the weed thing because it blows my mind that medical marijuana is now a thing. Yet it wasn't approved at the time, but rather on the FDA experimental list. The miracle drug was called Permavir. Don went from being in a lifeless comatose state, to back on his feet, off the vent and normal within two weeks of them injecting him with that medicine. I had never been so scared in my life as I was when Don was going through that. The site of his lifeless body and the thoughts of his death haunted me for years.

The bottom line is that it was a combination of Permavir and prayers that saved his life. I remember thinking to myself, "at least we'll never have to go through that again." I couldn't have been any more wrong in that assumption. For years, I would have nightmares that he didn't make it. I would reflect back on what happened at Wake Med Hospital in North Carolina and take comfort in the fact that I had witnessed a miracle. I hide from the shadows the entire ordeal cast on my soul. No one should witness a loved one in that position, ever.

It was at that time of my brother's recovery that I buried my attention on my book, *HERO* that I was working on. It was my first. Most said it would never get published. Every time I worked on it, it was to escape from the horrors I had seen. This became motivation to finish, and the book launched my writing career. It was the classic taking a negative and turning it into a positive. Writing can be a great escape.

★★★

There was no escape this time with Mom. We were about to enter the gates of pure Hell with no window in sight. It was a much different story this time too. My brother had never smoked a cigarette a day in his life, and was perfectly healthy before checking into the ICU. My Mom had 50 plus years of smoking under her belt and was easily one of the unhealthiest people I had ever met. She was running on pure stubbornness, grit and determination. Things were about to get very interesting.

I don't say any of this to be cruel or mock my mother, I say it because it was the reality of what we were facing. This was a woman whose body had been Hell for 61 plus years with every kind of nick and bruise you could think of. This was not going to be an easy task for a healthy person to bounce back from. Once Mom went on that vent, the chances of coming off it were slim to none.

I went home that night and tried to explain to Emily the exact severity of the situation and what we were facing. I explained that as long as Mom could stay off the vent, that she had a good chance to stay steady and eventually improve. It was crucial that she could breathe on her own and remain conscious. Emily understood, flashbacked with me to the Don trauma of 2009, and was fully understanding of how painful that was to go through. I gave Emily a hug and told her to hold on tight because I could already sense the coming days were going to be dicey. I let her know that I would take care of everything I could, and for her not to be afraid. Much easier said than done and I had no way to guarantee that, however, it is what husbands do.

In the early hours of the next morning my Dad got the call. Mom was going on the vent. Hell was set to begin.

CHAPTER FOUR

Hard times are when a man has worked at a job for thirty years – thirty years – and they give him a watch, kick him in the butt and say, 'Hey a computer took your place, daddy,' that's hard times! – Dusty Rhodes

Needing A Win

I must have walked back and forth from our bedroom to both of my daughters' bedrooms that night while everyone was asleep about a 100 times. Madelyn was sleeping through the night by that point, and Maggie was snoozing away in her big girl bed. I couldn't sleep, I couldn't eat, the sense of 'here were go again' was too much to shake. The only thing that was keeping me calm was looking at all three of my girls resting, peacefully innocent.

I just knew if Mom was going on that vent, there was a slim to none chance she was coming off it. Her health had deteriorated so much over her life, this would surely be a death sentence. I wasn't worried about myself, or even my Dad; we knew how to handle tough times. Lord knows we had been through plenty with Mom's health in the past, and always gotten through it. But this was different, much different.

Perhaps most of all, I was worried sick about Maggie. My little bean idolized Mom and the thought of having to possibly tell her how sick her 'Maga' was, was almost too much to bear. How do you even go about explaining that to a three-year-old? I kept telling Emily that we wouldn't inform Maggie of the severity of the situation until we absolutely had too. I hated watching Maggie cry. It killed me every time. It was no secret, even at only three years old that little bean ran my life. The same way her younger sister Madelyn eventually would as well. Maggie had recently said at the dinner table, "Mage Kee is my number one gal." Mom and her were super close. Mom had taught her so much about the Catholic faith, and especially about Mother Mary. Maggie may have been the only three-year-old in existence that knew how to say the entire rosary. She loved going to church with us and my parents as well.

You cannot bring children into the ICU, so there was no way she was going to be able to visit, and that was bad enough as Maggie was constantly asking to see her Maga. As long as Madelyn had a warm bottle and a comfy lap to hang out on, she would be fine, but Maggie was a different story. She is a tough little cookie, but I didn't want her to have to go through something like this at a young age. I realize it is a part of life, but Mom was only 61-years-old at the time. She had a lot still to see and Maggie was more than worth sticking around for. First days of school, graduations, school dances, ball games, dance recitals, all of it.

I know it sounds selfish but I don't care. I wanted her around to see Maggie's first day of school. To hear about her first kiss from a boy and see her graduate high school. Death was not an option. Maggie deserved her Maga to be around. As for the term 'Maga,' it is a word Maggie created when she first learned how to talk, calling both Emily's mother and my Mom

Maga. This was long before the entire Donald Trump craze.

★★★

Even before Dad called with the news a few hours later, I already knew. I could just sense Mom was headed for the vent. His call around 6 a.m. simply confirmed the pure Hell we were all about to encounter together. I couldn't believe we would have to go through it again after Don. The nightmare I never wanted to have to re-live was about to start once again. It was such a bitter pill to swallow first thing in the morning. I just wanted to vomit. I closed my eyes hard and squeezed, hoping to pop out of a dream. It wasn't. It was reality, and it was time to face it, head on.

I went to work that day without incident. Emily's parents watch the kids on Thursdays and Fridays so the entire ordeal of 'who is going to watch the girls today' was of no concern. My stomach was in constant knots all day, but oddly enough the work in front of me was a nice distraction. At times, it felt like the only thing I could control. My day job is constant work. There are no 'slow days.' As a bill collector, your plate is always full and your workload is always overloaded. Nine plus hours of hammering deadbeats about their bills that day actually felt kind of good. It was truly nice to get my mind off things. Who knew work would be such an amazing distraction, but it sure was!

I knew I was going to have to go straight from work to the hospital and see Mom in the comatose state on the vent. All day long I fought the images of Don in that same spot from dancing in my head. I couldn't face it again, could I? The first time with Donald had messed me up so bad, I just couldn't face it again. But again, it didn't matter if I wanted to; I had no choice. I almost went home after work and tried to hide from it all, but I knew I couldn't. I had been through so much the last couple of months. This was just another step on the journey I had to take. I didn't want to. I wanted to bury my head in a pillow somewhere and just sleep until it was over.

Work was over, and I was on my 60-minute drive back to Fairview Hospital. The long drive, as it always did, gave me a lot of time to think.

★★★

I'm not one to throw a pity party for myself, but this time around I couldn't help but reflect and almost sulk over the horrendous luck my life had been having. As I've stated, when you're first getting your start in the sports journalism world, you almost never find a paying job well enough to do it full time. You have to work two or three jobs just to make ends meet. For me, I didn't start sports writing until I was 32-years-old with a wife, kid, and baby on the way. So, for me, having a full-time job was the only way I was going to make it happen and justify being gone at night working as a writer.

I had nine books published, and did well, but it was never more than a few thousand dollars at the most, and that is counting book signings, royalty checks and paid speaking appearances per year. Sports writing would remain a pipe dream. I knew I could do it in what little spare time I had, but it was still a big deal to me and I was gaining a little bit of notoriety along the way. While all that was nice, and a dream come true in many ways, I still needed that eight to five to keep the lights on, cars running and family fed. It's true when they say writing is a labor of love. With all that being said, it was pretty damn important that I was bringing home a check for 80 hours of work every two weeks.

For a while, I was able to balance all of it nicely. Everything seemed fine as Emily had just given birth to Madelyn on September 10, 2016 (remember that date a little later). I was a proud father of two, author of nine published books, senior vice president of a sports website, loving husband to Emily and full time employee of what I thought was a reliable job. What could have possibly gone wrong?

Less than 10 days after Madelyn was born, the powers that be at the gas company pulled me in and fired me. To say I was stunned would be a drastic understatement. I was with the company five years and had the best numbers of the 90 collectors on staff. As recently as March of 2016 I had shattered the record for most money ever collected. It wasn't even close. I got a huge raise and everything seemed good to go. In the five years with the company, I hit goals every single month and had a spotless record. What the Hell could have possibly happened? I dared to ask for a transfer to a different department and it pissed off the wrong people. The next thing I knew, I was out of work.

Please allow me to back up a smidge and fill in a few important details as most people just don't get terminated without a backstory. As mentioned, in March I broke the company record for dollars collected in a three-month quarter. Most people would have loved it and bragged about it, not me, I wanted out! I loved working there and honestly thought I would retire there. I just didn't want to be a bill collector anymore; I was sick of it. As I said, I loved the company and had multiple friends in every single department. I tried to transfer to different departments multiple times, but every time it was blocked by my manager because I was pigeonholed. I would interview for a different department, land it, accept the offer and then have the manager of collections override it, keeping me put.

They had over 20 different departments I could transfer to, but it was useless. I tried one last time in June of 2016, right after the Cleveland Cavaliers won the championship. It was for my dream office job, as a recruiter. I would travel to schools, job fairs and present our company to perspective employees. I would also assist in the training of new employees. It was tailor-made for me. This time around I didn't even get to interview for the position as I was told I was "too personable" and it wasn't going to happen. Making matters worse, word leaked to my manager that I tried transferring out again, and I was immediately given severe punishment for it. They switched my supervisor, my route of accounts and pretty much spent each day making my life a living Hell for the next three months.

It was a nightmare, but I knew I had a kid on the way, five years in the can, and I needed to stick it out. I also had a ton of friends there, so I knew it couldn't be that bad if I just toughed it out. It didn't matter and I was let go shortly after the switch.

They were pissed I tried to transfer in June after breaking the record in March. They were looking for revenge and they got it. Right before this happened, in fact it was the week before this happened, I had been nominated by my peers for employee of the month for August. If that wasn't the final nail in my coffin, I'm not sure what was. I'll never forget as they were walking me out, the HR lady who loved me, the same lady who wanted me to work in recruiting hugged me tight. Her name was Tina and she whispered in my ear, "I'll make everything all right, just please don't sue us or we will be in a mess."

Upon losing my job, when I got home at 2 p.m., all three girls were asleep. It had been a long morning for them as well. I walked down to Little Clague Park by my house and just sat on a bench for a few minutes. How the Hell did all of this just happen?

Emily would be on unpaid maternity leave for the next 12 weeks per company policy. I suddenly had no income, and wasn't sure what the Hell was going to happen next. I thought to myself, this is the scariest thing I will ever have to face. A newborn to feed, a toddler getting bigger by the day, and a wife who I was going to have to sit down and tell her that her husband was in a major jam!

I closed my eyes and tried to breathe. I knew that if I could get through this, I could get through anything. I had been on TV and radio well over 200 times promoting my books. I had given over 100 speeches about my life, and never once did I feel the nerves. I pictured walking back in that door to face the girls who were now up.

As I figured, Emily totally understood and wasn't upset. I had never spent a dime of my royalty check money and was always diligent about saving my money. I knew we'd be okay for a few months while the bills came flying in.

But I refused to let the Gas Company off the hook for what they just did. I called a lawyer and also filed for unemployment within the next two hours.

Three weeks later, several large checks were sent to the house, and every Monday morning after that, the State of Ohio put a nice sized chunk in my bank account. I can't give away numbers, but I will just say that I was nicely taken care of as justice was served. It was also nice to be home with my girls during that stretch as well. It was almost like 'paid paternity leave.' The Gas Company may have screwed me, but because of their 'interesting move' and keeping my faith in the Lord, it ended up benefiting me greatly. It also put one in my favor in the good karma column.

The reason I bring up all of this job stuff is this, it made me stronger than I ever knew I could become. Close your eyes and think about it for a second: you're jobless, you have a new-born, a toddler, and a wife, with no income. Every morning you wake up wondering how the Hell you're going to feed them if you don't find something quick. That stretch before those large checks showed up at the house made me mentally tough.

I carried it with me every single day mentally since the moment it happened. I hated the people who fired me, and it drove me nuts to even think about it. I couldn't live with it as it burned me up inside and made me want to scream. God was about to show me, things could be and would be a lot worse. God was about to show me what really mattered. Life isn't always fair and the incident of losing my job set the tables for the biggest reminder of that to come.

I kept asking myself why the Lord was putting our family through this. What did I do? Who did I piss off? Why, God? He was teaching me. He was getting me ready for the battle still yet to come. If everything had been gravy, I may have never known how to handle a bad time. That stretch without a job was priming me for the ultimate battle.

★★★

I faced that battle firsthand two seconds after walking into Mom's hospital room that fateful Thursday afternoon and seeing my Mom lifeless. It was Don all over again, except this time, there was no miracle drug in the holster. I looked at Dad who was sitting there with the same saddened face I was sporting, and just said, "Well, here we go again, I'll grab the coffee." I mean, what the hell else was I going to say, it was a nightmare.

I walked back into the lobby to get the coffee and saw my cousins Tony, Gena and Frances all standing there waiting to visit as well. It was nice to have support, little did I know, that three would turn into almost 300 by the time it was all said and done. I was pissed Mom was sick. I was pissed I lost my job at the Gas Company, and I was pissed the Cleveland Clinic, a billion-dollar company refused to fix their broken coffee-maker for the third straight day in the ICU. I mean, really? Come the heck on! I'm clearly joking about the coffee thing, it *was* broken, but clearly there were far larger issues at hand.

My cousin Gena gave me a hug and told me it was okay to cry, but I wasn't ready yet, crying would come later. This was going to be a Hell of a lot tougher than looking for a new job. I just wanted a damn cup of coffee for Dad and I. It's the little things sometimes that really push you over the edge, and I was nearing it!

We needed a win. We needed a damn win. I was sick of losing since the past fall, and it was time for things to start going in our favor. I felt myself getting really pissed, to the point where I just wanted to punch someone. It was like every bad thing that happened would remind me of the BS the Gas Company pulled on me. I realized the two things had nothing to do with each other, but still, it didn't matter. They were easy to blame and be pissed at, so I directed my mental anger towards them any chance I had.

Being mad at the Gas Company helped me cope with the real problem going on. Horrible logic, but it was just how I felt at the time, and years later, still feel in many ways. But again, God's plan. So, for anyone reading this who was part of me being screwed there, thank you! Your relationship with the Devil, accepting evilness into your heart and business practices made me a stronger human being for my family, when they needed me the most.

★★★

Sadly, for Dad, seeing his wife in this type of life-threatening condition was nothing new. For him, it was the continuation of a nightmare that started nearly 40 years earlier. Dad and Mom continued to date past high school when one day they were walking through Great Northern Mall. Despite that Dad only had enough money in his pocket to afford a movie ticket, cup of coffee and stick of gum. he insisted they walk into the jewelry store. The clerk pulled out a few trays worth of rings and set them in front of the young couple. Until that point in her life, Mom only had two real pieces of jewelry: her class ring and a silver crucifix her friend, Sue, gave her for a birthday gift.

Dad was enthralled by all the rings on the trays and didn't know which one to choose, so he asked Mom to pick one out. She did, a modest white gold one and Dad asked the clerk how much it cost and how much he would have to put down to reserve it. The clerk said as little as one penny could be put down to reserve it, but you couldn't have it until fully paid for. Dad promptly took the rest of the change out of his pocket and reserved the ring.

Finally, the big day would come November 19, 1976. Their wedding day was beautiful and a dream come true. The wedding was held at St. Patrick's in West Park Cleveland. Here was this woman, that thought she would never find love, let alone get married and have children, and now Dad was doing everything he could to make those dreams happen for her and with her.

Dad really took a chance, and he wouldn't have done so if he wasn't truly in love. It was a fairytale story many thought they'd never see. Mom's story already gave hope to many with epilepsy: having the husband, the job and a future but she wasn't even close to being done yet.

Dad and Mom didn't wait long to try to start a family because they both wanted to be parents badly, plus when you have epilepsy you can never count on tomorrow. Each day is a gift because with such a serious condition you never know how ravaged your body might become. Mom and Dad knew the window to start a family would not be open long, and that many would frown upon it because of her condition. That did not stop them, and they kept trying.

It was August 16, 1977 which is the same week of the Assumption of the Blessed Mother into Heaven when the doctor called my parents with the good news. Despite the odds, Mom was now pregnant with my older brother Don.

When the call came in, the ringing bells set off a small seizure for Mom as Dad calmed her down and held her. He managed to answer the phone. Dad asked the nurse for the results but the nurse refused, saying that she could only talk to Mom about it. The nurse informed

Mom that the test came back pregnant. Mom instantly started celebrating by jumping up and down and screaming in joy. Dad took the phone and finished the conversation.

Mom and Dad went straight to the DeLuca home to share with Mom's family the wonderful news. Before they could even get the words out, Grandma knew exactly what was going on. She had been pregnant eight times, her oldest daughter Josephine had been pregnant three times, she knew just by looking at Mom's face that she was pregnant.

Everyone was excited! My grandparents had been told countless times that their daughter could never get pregnant. Her doctor had never hesitated to remind them that she shouldn't even try to have kids because it would kill her. Mom wanted children so badly she would even jokingly tell them that she wanted to have nine, so she could beat them by one.

So excited with the news of being parents, my parents went straight from my grandparents' home to the maternity store. When the sales girl came up to them, Mom couldn't resist telling her she was pregnant. She had lost all the weight from the previous medicine and was now back down to a size 3. She was so skinny that she didn't need the maternity clothes yet, but the excitement was still very much there. Mom was excited to be like her own mother, that she didn't care that the clothes wouldn't fit for months and still bought a bunch of them.

Because of her condition, she saw her doctor every three weeks during her pregnancy. The original due date was May 13, 1978. During the pregnancy her seizures were never under control but because of her large family she was never left alone. She stopped working as well because it was a very high-risk pregnancy. Grandma would pick her up every day, attend mass in the morning and spend the rest of the day with her until Dad came home from work. Her family was there to help her every step of the way.

On March 16, 1978, Donald Joseph McKee was born. He was tiny as expected for a two-month premature baby to be. He was five pounds at birth. The delivery team didn't hesitate to put oxygen on him to keep him breathing because he was not showing many signs of life. He didn't even cry like most babies do when born. They had to put Donald in the neonatal ICU (NICU) because he was starting to tremble and shake. He had all the medicines Mom was on in his system. He went from five pounds down to four in his first 24 hours of being alive. The doctors said he was going through withdrawals from the drugs Mom was on to help treat her epilepsy. It was a week before Mom would be cleared to leave the hospital. Her newborn son however was not healthy enough. It was a hard time period for my parents as daily they would have to look at the nursery in their home, and just wonder and dream as to when they could bring their baby home. It would be five weeks before Donald was healthy enough to come home.

It was a miracle that having the first child didn't kill her. But they loved being parents so much they wanted to try for one more. Mom felt that if God didn't want her to have another, then he wouldn't have planted a second seed into her life. Getting pregnant again would be very risky as the chance of mortality rose. There was a strong chance that she could get through the entire C-Section surgery but not make it through delivery. If this occurred, she would leave behind two children and a husband.

The other factor was that even if she got pregnant again, what would be the quality of life she could live? As a little boy growing up in the very early stages of his life, Don had to watch his mommy seizure right in front of him. Over and over again as a two-year, three-year and four-year-old, little Donald would have to witness the scary sadness as his mother convulsed on the ground and his eyes welled up with tears. No little boy should ever have to witness such a sad sight.

Despite the constant seizures, the constant pain and everything telling her that it would never happen again, Mom still tried to have another baby for the next several years as the agony continued. She and Dad had created life once, and they were determined to give Don a sibling. I for one, am very glad that they did because on January 14th, 1982 I came charging through! I was born a few weeks premature but as healthy and chunky as an ox. My parents were willing to make the ultimate sacrifice to bring me into the world, so I was determined to do anything possible to keep them in this world. My Mom fought for me, so I was going to fight for her. No more explanation needed, no matter how dark it got, I was going to scream from the rooftops and rally the troops to keep hope alive.

★★★

This was ringing in my mind as I went to find coffee, somewhere, anywhere, for the love of God, I was ready to walk to Columbia to get a darn coffee bean if that's what it took. That's when it hit me, I'll just walk to the cafeteria and ask for some. It was also then when my phone rang and it was my cousin David DeLuca calling.

I love David, he is not just a cousin, but one of my best friends in this world. They say sometimes cousins can be closer than brothers, and that is David and I to a tee. We're less than four years apart in age, and most times that difference isn't even noticeable. We spent so much time together for so many years, that his friends became my friends, and vice versa. David goes by the nickname Puka, and will be referred to as such for the rest of this book.

As mentioned, Puka and I were super close, we did everything together including season tickets to the Cavaliers for three seasons during LeBron James' original stay in Cleveland. You know, before he left twice in a blaze of glory each time. He used to bring me to these time share sales pitch things because he knew if he went alone he would cave to a pretty sales girl and buy one. But if we just sat through the miserable thing together, we'd get a free trip each time. So, sure enough, year one we sat through it and got a weekend in Vegas. Year two, we sat through it and got a free cruise. Year three, I had to work late causing me to miss it, and now Puka is the proud owner of 10-time share getaways. Her name was Becky.

To the best of my knowledge, he didn't know Mom was sick so I truly had no idea why he was calling and just figured it was one of his many random calls to me. This one was different, as Mom's life was apparently on its way to ending, our family had one just beginning. His brother's wife, Stephanie, had just given birth to their first child, Lincoln. Not only did I have a new second cousin, Lincoln, but he was born only minutes from where I was standing. The ICU unit at Fairview Hospital is not that far of a stroll from the birthing unit and before I knew it, I was on my way to hold my newest of kin.

Now, what makes this noteworthy and the reason I'm putting this in the story, is because it was a near miracle in itself. Without getting into the whole story and keeping things that need to remain private, just that, I will give you the Cliff Notes version of this story. My Uncle Joe and Aunt Karen had been married for 25 plus years before they got divorced. They had three kids, Puka, Matthew and Emily. The divorce was not pretty, and we never saw Emily again.

Matthew (Stephanie's husband), to his credit came around for years before breaking away from the DeLuca family. I hadn't seen him in five plus years but prayed all the time he may come back to us. He was one of my favorite cousins and I really missed him in my life. Puka stayed in touch with both his mom's side of the family but also ours. As mentioned, it had been years since I had last seen Matthew so I wasn't sure how this 'pop in' was going to go. Puka assured me it would be okay, so I went for it.

I knocked on the door and Matt answered it, grinning ear to ear. He had the glow of a new father and that is something that has to be seen or felt to understand just how special it is. His wife was beautiful and his little boy was a treasure. Minutes later I was holding little Lincoln and for the first time in a week, I was also smiling. A father of two, I know the strain on new parents, especially that first night, it can be brutal. With that knowledge, I knew to make my visit short. It was great to see Matt, meet his wife and hold his child. A much-needed moment of joy in a time of darkness.

As I walked back to the ICU, I just kept thinking about all the times my Mom had been in bad health situations and would bounce back. I mean, I was still pretty sure I would go home, go to bed, and wake up to a call from my Dad letting me know everything was all better. I was pretty naïve, or pretty stubborn, I'm not really sure.

As I walked back into the "death unit," I noticed that it was a little fuller than when I had left. Tony, Gena and Frances, my three oldest cousins were still there, but so was Don. He must have driven all day, but he was there and in the room with Mom and Dad. It was nice to see him, as seeing your whole family back together is a great feeling, despite the fact that one member was pretty much dead, staying alive by a giant tube and hooks all over her body and down her throat. I left him alone with Dad so he could fill my brother in on how serious things had gotten in just the last couple of hours.

I sat down with my cousins and told them who I had just seen and who I had just held in my arms. They couldn't believe what I was telling them and almost seemed in joyous disbelief in the hopes they could meet little Lincoln next. Sadly, I had to pop the balloon of hope quickly as Matt had let me know that they wouldn't be taking any more visitors.

I eventually walked back in Mom's room, and gave her a kiss on the forehead, whispering some words of encouragement in her ears as well. I would always start with, "I know you can hear me, so listen up and listen clearly." They say people in medically-induced comas can't hear you, but I don't buy that theory at all. They may not remember it afterwards, but I would bet anything that they can hear you in the heart of the moment. As I was talking with her, pleading for her to get better, I couldn't take my eyes off the tiny round knob that would go on to symbolize hope, faith and possible death. A tiny round knob that would become the source of a movement and hopeful progress. There's a dial on the vent, it tells you how much oxygen the patient is relying on from the machine to take each breath, and how much the patient is breathing on their own. Right now, the machine was doing 100% of the work and Mom was taking 0% of her own breaths. It doesn't get any worse than that. I swear to God I just wanted to reach over to the dial and turn it to 50/50 and let my Mom shock everyone. I knew she had it in her to try it, but at that point, it was still day one on the vent, and we had to let it play out. She could only be on it so long. The clock was ticking.

I walked over to Dad and gave him a giant hug. It was crazy because the last time I hugged Dad was also in a hospital room. It was in the same hospital Fairview as well, except it was in the birthing unit moments after Madelyn was born. My dad and I were very close, in many ways. He wasn't just my dad, but also my mentor and my closest friend. He was a role model, and if I was ever in a jam, he was the first person I would call.

Remember when I said remember the date September 10, 2016? That's because it was UFC 203 being held at Quicken Loans Arena in Cleveland. I already know what you're saying too, what the Hell does that have to do with anything? Simple, I was there, cage side covering the event, living out a dream that was coming true. Meanwhile, Emily who was nine months pregnant went into labor. Being a good 25 plus minutes away, I couldn't get there fast enough, so Dad sped her to the hospital while I hauled arse from the event to get to Fairview. Luckily, I made it by six minutes as Madelyn didn't waste any time making her presence felt. My Dad was in the room when she was born, he never left. I tell this story because of how quickly things can change in the exact same place. In September I embraced my Dad with joy as my new child came into the world. A few months later, we embraced with the specter of death in the air. Same building, same two people, much different moment.

I never cried when I lost my job. I never cried when I got out of bed for two months straight, every day looking for a new job, wondering what was next with my life. I just let it pile up and pile up until one day, it was going to all come out at once. That day was right now! I walked into the ICU lobby, buried my head in my legs and just let it out. I finally snapped; it was the lowest point of my life. Everything hit me at once. In my mind I envisioned my brother on the vent; I envisioned my mom on the vent; my Uncle Pete in the coffin in 2004; and the HR lady from The Gas Company walking me out the door and I finally snapped.

I was so pissed I lost my job. I was so pissed Mom was in this bad spot. I was so pissed that my Grandparents were possibly going to lose their third child (Peter 2004 and Josephine 2010). That anger turned into sadness and emotion and I couldn't hold it in anymore. I cried for a good five minutes straight. I couldn't stop, it truly was everything at once. Cousin Gena gave me a long hug and told me it was okay to cry, that I had to stop holding it in for so long. She was right, and I instantly felt better. It may have been okay to let it out finally after all.

Even with that said however, I swore to myself after that, I wouldn't cry again until my Mom was up walking and talking again, or dead. No in-between. I would let everyone cry but I was going to be the pillar of strength. That was all there was to it. I'd be there for everyone else but look for mercy from no one. People around me would see the strongest and most fearless version of Vince McKee that they had ever seen. I would become someone everyone could be proud of. The breakdown was over, and it was time to lead the way. I would not be denied as I was about to have the largest pair of shoulders possible. I was done with losing, enough was enough and the world was about to find out.

CHAPTER FIVE

God is great indeed,
If you believe, in the everlife
Yeah we gotta
Make some sense of the piece that's not defined
And if you just hold on, I won't let you fall
We can make it through the storms and the
winds of change

– 'Lonely Road of Faith'
lyrics by Kid Rock

The Meeting

Friday morning April 21, 2017 had arrived. The Cavaliers were fresh off a 20 plus point comeback to defeat the Indiana Pacers the night before in Game Three of their first-round playoff series. The Cleveland Browns were less than a week away from picking first overall in the NFL draft. The Cleveland Indians were building what would become a comfortable lead in the American League Central Division, but none of that would mean anything to me that morning.

Normally a sports junkie, all of that would have made my Friday morning amazing, but on this day, I'll say it again – I couldn't care less.

Normally those three areas of sports would be the first thing I would check each morning before I even brushed my teeth. This time the alarm went off, and I was checking my phone for a much different reason. I wasn't checking scores; I was checking to make sure I didn't miss any calls letting me know Mom was alive or dead. It wasn't a game of balls and strikes, or three pointers and slam dunks, it was the ultimate game of life or death, and I couldn't afford another loss.

There weren't any missed calls, there weren't any missed text messages or anything of the sort. Little did I know, that would be the last morning my phone would not be going berserk for the next several weeks. We had done a good job keeping things off social media and under wraps for the most part, but all of that was about to change dramatically.

Driving to work the talk on the radio was all about the upcoming NFL draft as well as the

Cavaliers big comeback the night before, but I couldn't concentrate on sports talk, as much as I had wanted to. Instead, I just kept picturing Mom lying motionless as the machines kept her going. I kept just kept picturing Dad praying by her bedside. His faith was unwavering and always strong in any situation.

Work that morning seemed to go by quick as I had kept my mind focused on the task in front of me. Collecting money from people who didn't want to pay it. That seemed the simplest of tasks at that point. I actually looked forward to being at work to get my mind off things. While not the dream job, it was '*a*' job, and I was happy to have the money every two weeks and the distraction that day.

That would change on the drop of a dime when I got a call from Don that things had in fact managed to worsen through the night. This was the first I was hearing of it and it was a punch to the gut. Apparently, Dr. Salem, the doctor in charge of the portion of the ICU, had been checking out my Mom that morning and she looked worse than ever. It was no longer just double pneumonia causing her not to be able to breathe, but something much worse, ARDS.

Acute respiratory distress syndrome (ARDS) is a rapidly progressive disease occurring in critically ill patients. The main complication in ARDS is that fluid leaks into the lungs making breathing difficult or impossible. Few have ever come back from it once diagnosed, for many it is a death sentence.

Mom's already destroyed lungs from 40 years of smoking, were now having fluid rapidly fill them up to the point it was about to kill her. Every time my Dad or I would say, 'well, not sure it can get worse,' it found a way to do so. This news of ARDS was devastating, it pretty much took any ray of hope and turned the light off on it. So now the question was, how much longer do we keep her on the vent when the chances at a recovery didn't seem very possible? Thus, the reason for Don's call as Dr. Salem wanted an emergency meeting called with Dad, Donald and me.

That was it for me. Enough of keeping things quiet, I had to let people know what was going on and quickly. I sent a mass text to my cousins. I had 17 first cousins on my Mom's side, but only sent the text to a representative of each family. Remember, Mom had seven siblings, six of which had children, thus the 19 total grandchildren. I knew if I got the word out to Puka, my cousin Annie Morino, my cousin Nicole Eliseo and my cousin Gena, they would take care of the rest.

I also knew full well what this meeting was going to be about. Take her off the vent and let her die, or keep her on it and hope for a miracle? My mind was already made up to push for a miracle, but it was crucial that we heard everything the doctor had to say.

It wasn't more than 45 seconds after sending that text to my cousins about the emergency meeting that I got a call from both Annie and Puka. I let them know exactly what was going on and the extent of it. Until then most of my family knew nothing, other than, 'Maria is sick.' To the best of my knowledge that was about it. That was about to also change, dramatically.

The DeLuca family sticks together like no cast and crew you've ever seen. We will take over a waiting room in minutes. There is no better example of this than when I walked off the elevator into the ICU waiting room and saw no less then 30 plus DeLuca's sitting there waiting on me to arrive so the meeting with the doctor could begin. Apparently, everyone had a shorter drive than my 60 minutes from Akron to get to the hospital. School was out that week for Easter Break, so even the cousins of mine who go to school, were out on break and at the hospital.

Two seconds off the elevator and into the waiting room, I noticed my wife Emily along with my cousin Gena and her two girls; my cousin Frances and her husband Mike; Uncle Joey and Puka; Aunt Rose, her husband Sylvie and her daughter Nicole along with best friend Dawn. My cousin Tony, his partner Rick and their two children Monterra and Ronell. Uncle Jimmy and his wife Elsa along with their son, Joe. Aunt Franny with her husband Uncle Matt and their kids Annie, Anthony and Annamarie. My aunt Anna and her four boys Emerson,

Chris, Joe and Gabriel. My Grandparents along with my grandmas' sister, Aunt Fran and her son, Michael. My Mom's closest friends, Jenny Shade and Cathy Wade. Her other best friend, Camille, would have been there but she was in California at the time preparing to fly home.

That is 34 people right there who dropped what they were doing and rushed to the hospital. Think about that for a second. In pretty much the drop of a hat, over 30 people showed up in a waiting room at the ICU in the middle of the afternoon. More people would have been there too if they could have left work or didn't live out of town. 34 was a nice sized number, but it was just beginning, more on that later.

Things were getting serious, dead serious and a gigantic decision was looming. There were immediate questions as to who would enter the "big meeting" with the doctor to decide Mom's fate. Clearly it would be Dad, Donald and I, along with our spouses. Abbie was still in North Carolina but I was blessed to have Emily there. It was also agreed that my cousins, Tony and Gena who both worked in the medical field, would come in the room with us for any needed guidance. It was a special request of my Dad so I didn't fight it. Whatever was going to make him feel comfortable at that point was fine with me.

When Dr. Salem came out to get us to go in the special meeting room, he had a look on his face as to say, 'who the hell are all these people?' I cannot imagine a doctor has ever walked into a scene like that on a Friday afternoon in the spring. Or in any season for that matter. I grabbed a pen and notepad out of Emily's purse, I thought it would be important to write as many things down as possible while the doctor was talking. I wasn't going to leave a stone unturned or a question unasked. Others may have gone into that room thinking they were about to plan a funeral, I went into that room determined to hear every viable option possible to save my mother's life. I didn't care if I became Fairview Hospital's biggest pain in the arse, I would become a human enema if it meant keeping my Mom alive.

★★★

Unfortunately for my Dad, and quite sad honestly, this was not the first time he had to go into an emergency meeting to decide my Mom's health future. The last time however was 34 years prior and for much different reasons. Shortly after I was born, Mom started having three grand mal seizures a day, the most in her life, and the petite mal were constant in between. The constant seizures left her a vegetable most of the time, having to sit on pads so she wouldn't hurt herself too bad with the seizures. She wasn't able to take care of her new baby, me, and things just kept getting worse.

Mom and Dad arrived at 6p.m. on March 28, 1983 in Dr. Victor Victoroff's office alongside of my grandparents. Dr. Victoroff was a tall man, with straight white hair and thick black glasses. He never let the fact that he had the same first and last name throw him. He was determined and smart. The good doctor asked questions to everyone in the room for nearly a half hour straight as he examined her. He was amazed that after the first 27 years of her life, with everything she went through that she was even able to walk. He explained that the only thing he thought they should do to make the seizures stop was brain surgery. He stated that all the medicine in the world was not going to help. They had tried everything and brain surgery was the last option.

Dr. Victoroff went on to explain that there was a hospital in Montreal, Canada called the Montreal Neurological Institute that was partnered with the McGill University, and they were the only ones able to do the very risky and controversial surgery. It was the top medical college in the world. Some of its graduates had won the Nobel Peace Prize for producing some of the top equipment in the medical fields in the world and their top priority was finding a cure for brain disease. It also had a good history of successful brain surgeries as the first ever successful one was done there.

The concern was great as brain surgery at that time was still pretty much unheard of and the risks were heavy. The casualty rate was high of people dying during the surgery, and slightly afterwards. Just like in that meeting room in Fairview, back then my parents had a hell of a decision on their hands. They went for the surgery. It was either live life as a vegetable, or go for the miracle – eerily similar to the choice we were about to have. They were Montreal bound later that month.

They would eventually arrive at the hospital which was very big and very clean. It was also very old. It was quiet as well, with wide hallways but not very much hustle and bustle. The nurse showed Mom her room in the ward. It almost appeared to be the docks at a military camp. As each ward had two rows of beds, ten each lined up with small foot lockers at the bed of each one. There was a small night table next to each bed as well. It was very different because as a patient you went to the hospital café for your meals, you had to wash your own clothes and dress up in formal wear every morning unless there was a test scheduled to take place first thing in the morning then you could stay in your gown. The diversity of the patients was also great as in Mom's ward alone, a room filled with 20 patients and only three of them were actually from Canada. The rest had come from all over the world.

Every test they did they explained what they were doing by performing it on another patient first so the patient could better understand the reasoning behind it. This allowed the patient to ask plenty of questions as well. For the first two weeks all the tests were done which allowed Mom still to be able to walk to the area of the huge hospital to have them done. Other times, the testing would be done at McGill University and the patients would be driven over. The testing was incredibly unique, using everything from ink blot tests to card games to study how her brain worked. The doctors, students and nurses would write down and study her every move.

Dr. William Fiendel was the Chief of Staff and the Dean of the McGill University. He was of medium height with blue eyes, white hair, slightly balding and a calm demeanor. Dr. Fiendel explained to Mom that he was the man with God's help who would stop the horrible seizures. He also explained to her the reason for all the testing she had been going through. He and his team of doctors had been studying the results of each test so he could completely understand exactly how her brain worked.

They had taken Maria off her medicine while there as well, so they could see her brain in its natural element. This caused her seizures to be out of control and constant. They were getting stronger and larger each time. While she was having hers at times she would look over and other patients were having them as well. It was the first time she had to witness someone else go through the hell that had plagued her life. For the first time, she saw how horrible they were to watch. All she could think of was her poor husband and son, having to watch her go through that so many times.

After she was cleaned up from the seizure and resting comfortably trying to recover, her next test was in toughness and mental fortitude. A man with a pair of clippers walked into the room: it was haircut time. He lifted a towel off a tray, and sure enough sitting there was a pair of shiny new electric clippers, primed and ready to shave her head clean. He also had a straight edge razor and shaving cream. At the time, Mom's hair was very long, all the way past her shoulders and down to the midpoint of her back. The barber put it into ponytail form and cut it. He cut as much as he could, but the hair was so thick it would eventually take the electric razors to finish the job and give Mom her first ever buzz cut.

A haircut, an enema, a salt bath, none of it mattered compared to the hell she had been through and the hell still yet to come the next day. After the last bath, Maria returned to her room and prepped to be strapped in for the night. She got under the sheets and propped the bed upright so she could see Dad when he walked in. Dad knew exactly what to do and also what to bring to help Mom be at ease the eve before the most important day of her life. He brought a bunch of pictures from home, along with a cassette tape with all the voices from her family members and children on it talking to her. It was a special message from Don that really touched her. Her young son reminded her how much he loved her and wanted her to come home. He told her that he would take care of her and how much he missed her. At only five years old, it was a lot for Don to have to go through.

As Mom fell asleep that night, the angels in heaven were working overtime watching over her and preparing her soul for its greatest journey. The name of and destination of that journey was freedom. She had gone her whole life emotionally, physically and mentally crippled from a condition that no human being should ever have to endure. And now, after over a quarter of a century of dealing with hell, she would have her chance to fight against the greatest villain in her life. It was a battle with the greatest prize on the line. Once again that prize was freedom. Freedom from the prison epilepsy had held her body, mind and soul captive for so many years prior.

She was over 10,000 miles away from her bed, away from her sons, her parents and the only place she ever knew as home. She was away from those who supported her. Everything was behind her and what awaited her could be glorious if she could get there. But like a wise man once said, sometimes it's hell getting to heaven. Her head was going to be cut open, not only that but it would be with a drill and a saw with no Novocain.

She had a lifetime of seizures, of torment, of pissing herself, doctors, hospitals, embarrassment and never knowing when the next attack would occur. A lifetime of being scared, wondering when the hell it would come back, when the pain would ever let up. Not even end, but simply give her a pain free day. For the first 99 percent of her life, it seemed as though that would never occur. Now, she was in Canada, surrounded by geniuses and about to take the chance of a lifetime. This was it, one more trip to hell for a chance at heaven.

★★★

All of that was on Dad's mind in April of 2017, 24 years later, as we walked in the room with Tony, Gena, Donald and Emily to sit with

Dr. Salem and hear just how bad Mom was doing. This was no longer 1983 where a miracle surgery could possibly save her life. This was 2017, 34 years later with a fate looking every bit as bleak.

Dr. Salem began to speak as I began to write the news as, not good…

CHAPTER SIX

'Don't use social media to impress, use it to impact' – Dave Willis

Going Viral

As a writer there is no better news to get than, 'your article just went viral.' The term means that thousands and sometimes even millions of people read your article or saw your tweet. It's a big deal and can happen from something small or huge. There really is no rhyme or reason to it.

I've written articles that took me hours, that I poured my soul into and did hours upon hours of research that got very few, if any views. I've written other articles that took me two minutes and went viral. You just never know.

The American public is great, extremely fascinating, but sometimes a frustrating bunch. Sometimes things that seem like can't miss, do exactly that. Other times, you throw something against the wall last second out of desperation and people love it. Case in point, I worked for years on a book called, *Ohio Warriors*. In my humble opinion, it is the best book I've ever written by far. I interviewed some of the greatest fighters in the world of MMA and boxing to ever come out of Ohio, and it came out excellent. It was easily the most fun I ever had writing a book as well. It was a guilty pleasure book, but one that was very well done! I'm extremely proud of Ohio Warriors and would urge everyone to buy it! This book was as can't miss as can't miss got. There were ZERO books ever written with this kind of backup to them. None to come out of Ohio, and pretty much no articles ever written either that combined the stories and quotes of so many fighters. I had multiple hour-long interviews with men such as Stipe Miocic, Mike Goldberg, Ray Boom Boom Mancini, Shawn Showtime Porter, and Gray Maynard just to name a few of many. The book was set to come out in June of 2015, and until that point, my best seller was Cleveland's Finest with well over 20,000 sold. I thought for sure that this would blow that out of the water because of how good it was; how unique it was and quite frankly, it was just pretty damn fun to read and write.

It sold 32 copies. Let that sink in for a second. 32 copies ... two plus years of my life down the drain for 32 copies. The biggest problem was that even though the people in the book enjoyed being honored in it, only one of them actually helped promote it. The one person was Vonda Ward, who is perhaps the sweetest athlete and most incredible human being I've ever met. The other painful lesson I learned from the debacle was that fight fans don't like to read about fights. They just want to watch them. So maybe if it was a documentary done audio style or visual style, it would have sold 64 copies. Oh well, go figure! All of my other books sold thousands of copies each, I guess 8 out of 9 isn't too shabby.

I use this example because it goes to show that you never know what is going to pull at a heart string. What is going to make people care and what will get a reaction out of someone. What can a person relate to? If they had a person in their family die from cancer, then they are more likely to walk in a cancer walk, or donate money. It is a sad fact, but a true one.

I started this book off by telling you how a man was so desperate for attention and suffering from mental problems, that he literally shot and killed someone he didn't even know on social media. Facebook, Twitter and other formats can be deadly. They can break up marriages; they can start fights, and they can tear people down. I still say that Facebook's biggest monetary beneficiary are marriage counsellors and divorce lawyers.

Sadly, social media is not always used for the right reasons of taking pictures of your loved ones, and yes, even pets and food. Prayer chains are a big deal on social media as well, and most times it will get a few likes and comments. Lucky for the McKee bunch, we were about to see the wonders of social media for the good reasons. We'll get to that in a second, first we had to endure some very bad news.

★★★

As Dr. Salem began to speak, the news was not very good, in fact it was downright awful. The chances of my mom making it were now slim to none and he didn't shy away from letting us know that – to his credit. He is a doctor and by law they must tell you 100% fact. He didn't sugarcoat anything, and that is what great doctors do. They tell you how it is and deal with the facts.

My mom's lungs were pretty much shot to hell from years of smoking abuse and countless other illness that plagued her. When he showed us the X-ray it was easy to tell how bad they were. I mean, even without the old red pen to circle the bad parts, you could still see the problems crystal clear. I was desperate and even offered to give her one of my lungs to help matters out, but I was quickly told that her body was in such terrible condition that she couldn't survive any surgery, let alone a lung transplant. Looking back on it now, I'm pretty sure my Dad and Emily would have never allowed me to do that anyway, but at that moment I was desperate.

The doctor went on to explain that she could only stay on that vent 14 days and the clock was ticking quickly. She went on the thing April 18 and that pretty much made May 2nd the due or die date. And yes, I used that term for a reason. No vent, means no breath, and no breath means death.

My Dad asked Dr. Salem for a percentage, and he said at best it was around 15% that Mom may start to improve to the point we could take her off the vent and breathe with the assistance of an oxygen tank and mask. He said this because it was clear my mother would never again breathe on her own. Even by some fluke if she got off the vent, she would be one of those people you see at the bingo hall, grocery store or church with a small oxygen tank by their side and tubes up their nose. Yep, the future was looking bleak no matter how you wanted to slice it.

My Uncle Joey who had slid into the room, joining Emily, myself, Donald, Tony, Gena and my Dad, was the next to ask a question. His is one I can't remember; I just recall the answer being bleak and Emily starting to cry. At that point, I looked over and everyone was crying, except my Dad. He just stared ahead in disbelief and looked like a deer in the headlights. You could see he was heartbroken and reality was starting to settle in. It was at this point that something in my head snapped. I was done losing. I was done listening to bad news and just taking it. I was done feeling helpless in a dire situation and watching everyone around me hurt. I took matters into my own hands and began to fight like hell.

I know what you're saying, you're thinking that what in the hell could this guy do? It was up to the medical field and the experts to make the decisions. And I get that, and you have every right to think I'm full of myself, but I swear to God, from that moment forward I was done taking no for an answer and began to take charge. Dad was too scared and he badly wanted a mouthpiece. Someone who could fight for him and Mom. I was going to be that mouthpiece and I didn't give two craps if I pissed anyone off along the way. If it meant getting tossed out of a hospital then I was going to do it.

Lucky for me, Dr. Salem seemed to really like me and listened to my questions and suggestions. As this story goes on, you will see a bond develop behind the scenes that proved to be a difference maker several times over. Dr. Salem was a great man willing to try anything, and also didn't want to give up.

As the meeting was about to breakup, I asked Dr. Salem that with the days growing short of how long she could stay on the vent, why not try lowering the amount of oxygen the machine was cranking in her? I pleaded and begged that we could lower it down to 90% and see if her body could produce that extra 10%? what was the worst that could have happened? If it didn't work, you crank it back up to 100% and you try again the next day. Dr. Salem agreed and asked Dad if that was his wish too, it was, so we went for it. I often times felt like Dad was much too reliant on what the medical "experts" were telling him and not comfortable with demanding things. It was his wife after all and what he said should go.

Mom was going to die, the chances of survival were slim, why not fire every bullet you have in that gun on the way out the door? It was a message that I pumped in my Dad's brain over and over again as the days would pass. *Go for broke!*

As we walked back into the ICU waiting room, the room had grown from 40 plus family and friends to 60 plus within minutes, with even more people parking their car in the garage. All of them wanted answers and they wanted them now. I looked at Dad waiting for him to talk. He wasn't ready and couldn't bring himself to do it. I looked over at cousin Tony, who quickly told me it wasn't his place as her nephew, and that either Donald or I should address everyone. Don wasn't in the mood to do it, so I took it upon myself to become the mouthpiece for the family moving forward. It wasn't a role I envisioned moments earlier, but one I was more than willing to try.

I've been watching pro wrestling since I was four years old. For 30 plus years I would mimic the wrestlers when they gave their promos. I can't begin to tell you how many Bret Hart, The Rock, Macho Man, Steve Austin and Hulk Hogan promos I recited word for word in my bathroom mirror over the years. In fact, my first book, *HERO*, was titled after a portion of a Bret Hart speech from the summer of 97 when he thanked Canada for still letting him be their hero.

Pro wrestling and Rocky movies took a large part in the writer I was, the parent I wanted to be and the son I always was. People may think it is crazy but between Rocky movies and pro wrestling you have a lifetime of inspirational moments and quotes that could get you through anything. The funny thing is that my mom hated pro wrestling, but it would be that exact industry that I pulled quotes and terms from to rally people to save her life with prayer. With that knowledge in the back of my mind, and over 60 sets of eyeballs and ears now staring a hole through me, desperate for hope, desperate for good news, I began my speech.

‘I won’t lie to anyone, and I won’t provide any false hope. The DeLuca family has been blessed to see many miracles in our time, and we are in need of another one. Chances are, you will be burying your aunt, your sister, your daughter, your niece, your cousin and your friend very shortly in the coming weeks. Dr. Salem has gone into detail explaining what ARDS is, and it doesn’t look good for Mom. Right now, they are pumping her full of air with the vent, and it is the only thing keeping her from dying in that bed.

That is not good, that is not a way to go through life, and quite frankly she only has 12 days left before they remove her from that vent, and let her die. This is as real as real gets. This is not a nightmare, but a horrific reality we must all now face together.

My mom, your aunt, your sister, your daughter, your friend, your niece and cousin will die. Any result other than that, will be a miracle. With that being said, no one, and I mean *no one* is going to take away our hope and our will as a family. No medical record, no diagnosis and no odds can keep you from having hope and faith in God. It is his will, my mom's fate is in his hands but can be willed by *you*!

If we all pull together, and pray, and continue to spread the word for needed prayers *anything* can happen. While we stand here now in pain, in despair, there is nothing keeping us from rallying around each other and my mom. We win as a team, and we lose as a team. Now is our time to call on every prayer, every wish and every hope you've ever had in you.

Now is the time to say, "screw ARDS," this one is in *our* hands. No one, and I mean *no one* can tell you how hard to fight, and how hard to pray. Our time with my mom appears to be coming to an end, but it doesn't have to, without a fight. Now I'm going to fight, so who wants to fight with me?'

My grandmother's sister, Aunt Fran, was there and asked everyone to stay in the same circle they gathered in to hear me speak. She was excellent as she began a prayer and told me that no matter what happened, God's will would be done.

Aunt Fran was always such a soothing voice in any sorrowful moment. I have nothing but respect for my Great Aunt Fran who much like my own grandmother, always put everyone else first and lives her life with love. Maybe there is something about the name Frances, as I've received some of my best advice in life from my Aunt Franny, and also my cousin Frances.

So, as reality suddenly sunk in, so did hunger. I myself wasn't very hungry and I was rapidly losing weight from stress and no appetite, but I was aware that the people around me needed to eat. I told my brother, he should order some pizzas for everyone who would be sticking around the ICU waiting room for the rest of the day. He joked and said, 'why should I do it? You're the one with all the experience ordering large amounts of pizza.' This was a wisecrack about a time in my youth that will forever live in infamy.

★★★

When I was in high school, I didn't drink or smoke, or even play a ton of video games. I was creative with my high jinks and that included one rainy night in March of 1999. My parents were out at a wedding and my brother was off with his girlfriend. My friends, Joe and Allen, were over when I came up with the bright idea to order pizza. But the tasty treat would not be for us, oh no, far from it.

There was this little old lady who lived across the street from us on the corner. For whatever reason she never had the light on for Halloween. Her house was a "no candy zone." It was petty, but I didn't forget that I figured if she didn't like candy, it was time to see if she liked pizza. We proceeded to order two large pizza's, crazy bread and multiple two liters of soda from each pizza chain in a delivery radius. We said we would pay in cash. Keep in mind, this was 1999, so these types of things were much easier to pull off than they are now. If the place served it, we'd throw in wings and salad too. We spaced it out so each pizza order would show up in five-minute intervals of one another. Although at one point, the Pizza Hut guy and Dominos guy showed up at the same time. That in itself made what was about to happen next, almost worth it. Oh, and did I mention it was pouring rain?

As my friends and I watched from behind the curtains, laughing every step of the way, things became really serious very fast as two North Olmsted police cars came rolling up my driveway. Despite the invention of caller ID, not being as prevalent back then, the woman saw one of us run outside and write down her address from our front yard. Super criminals we were not. With that being said, she kept track of every pizza chain to show up and every pissed off delivery driver who just got stiffed on the order. It totaled 13 in all and none of them were very happy about it. She called each pizza place, gave them our address, and then called the police and pressed harassment charges.

For the next 45 minutes it was one pizza guy showing up at our house dropping off the pizza after another. The punishment was having to apologize to each pizza delivery man, and then apologize to the woman we harassed. Oh yeah, we had to pay for the food too. A nice $300 plus bill.

★★★

As spot on and funny as Donald's joke was, I still wasn't in the mood to eat. I ended up sticking around until about 2a.m. that night, which became the normal. People came in and out, and for the day we counted right around 121 visitors in all. It was weird in a way, almost like a wake while the person was still alive. As nice as it was to receive that kind of support, it was still rough as people spoke to Dad with such sympathy. It was as if hope just didn't exist for them, and they knew after one look at her that it was over.

Finally, it was time to go. No less than three people were checked into the ICU that day who died. It was so weird watching people I didn't even know go through such pain as they lost loved ones, meanwhile my mom was still plugging away.

With the next day being Saturday, I knew Emily would be home so I could spend as much time at the hospital with my Dad and brother as needed. However, that would have to start in the early afternoon as I had two bookings in the morning that day. Two different libraries had booked me to give my talk that I do. The talk I give is one of inspiration as it covers my journey as a sportswriter and author of nine books. It's an inspirational message telling people that no matter how many obstacles may be in your lives' path, that if you work hard and continue to move forward, anything can happen.

***

I usually take the bookings at religious events, schools, libraries and large sports themed gatherings. It is a good speech that I enjoy giving and most times comes with a short book signing afterwards. This day was different however, as my mind was everywhere else but focusing on a talk.

As I pulled into the first parking lot that day, I tried to figure out how I could possibly compose myself with so much going on. I called one of my mom's closest friends, Camille. She was someone who I have grown to admire and become close with myself. She was vacationing in California at the time, and I felt bad calling so early but knew she would understand. Camille is one of those people who is a saint on Earth. It is crazy to think sometimes, but that is one area of my mom's life that never lacked. She had some of the closest and best friends a human being could ask for. Between Camille, Jenny, Cathy Wade and Sue, just to name a few, my mom had so much support in the friendship department!

Camille is one of the people I could trust and count on to always set me straight with encouragement or tough love. One time I had a book singing in a barn, and she was the only person to show up. I'm not mad about it, I mean, it was a barn for Pete's sake. She was always there for me, and always with great advice. She made me feel like a winner at life, and someone who truly believed in me because they wanted to and not because they had to. There were so many times in my writing career that I wanted to give up. So many times, that 'KEE On Sports Media Group' seemed like a pipe dream that would never happen. Camille was at the top of the list of people who would encourage me and never let me give up.

Camille was a mess and holding back tears. She had spoken with Dad and he filled her in pretty good. When I mentioned to her that I was about to give a speech at multiple libraries, she immediately perked up and went into encouragement mode. She told me to focus and believe in myself. She had heard over 20 of my talks and was my biggest fan. She knew exactly what to say to help me choke back the tears and focus on the task at hand. It was classic Camille and once again one of the biggest reasons I absolutely love her!

After I hung up the phone, it dawned on me what library I was at that morning. It was the one in West Park which I had grown up going to, before we moved to North Olmsted. It was also the site of the infamous, "milkshake debacle." A story that wasn't one of my father's best moments, but one worth telling none the less.

★★★

In the summer of 1988, the Cleveland Indians were so bad that they had to constantly run local promotions for free tickets just to get people to show up. One of those promotions was to open up a library card, and get two free tickets. Dad took me to the West Park Library and we did exactly that. Ironically enough, even though we were there to get free tickets, I would grow up loving to read and write. Perhaps that was the start of it, who really knows but that day was all about baseball.

What stands out about this day, and I can clearly remember this 30 years later, was the librarian lecturing my father and I for over an hour. She went on and on about the importance of book safety and how we must never drink liquids or eat food anywhere near a library book. This woman had been working there since the

1940s. She was so old she read the Bible just to reminisce. I mean, she was so old she had a front row seat at the big fight between David and Goliath. She made Mrs. Howell from Gilligan's Island look like a hot young thing.

Trust me, I get it, no food near a book that you don't own. If you spill something on it, you've now ruined a book that doesn't even belong to you. I have learned my lesson the hard way over the years when people ask to 'borrow' one of my books and it comes back destroyed. People are so cheap.

It wouldn't have been that big of a deal but as we were coming home from the game that night it was the typical mid-August thunderstorm in Cleveland. As I recall, the summer of 1988 is one of the hottest ones on record. We didn't have air conditioning in our Cleveland house so all the windows were open. Again, normally this wouldn't even be that big of a deal had it not been for the bookcase in which the books we checked out that day were sitting on top of. The bookcase was positioned up against the window and you don't have to be a rocket scientist to figure out what happened next.

The rain soaked the books, the next day when we realized it, they were already dry and had ballooned up like only wet carboard or paper can. They were ruined with no chance of being fixed. As Dad and I looked at the ruined books, and then at each other, not a word was uttered, until my Dad finally said, 'that crusty old librarian is going to be pissed.'

Like always, my Dad thought quick on his feet, and he hatched quite the plan to get us out of this little snafu. He told me to get in the car and he would handle everything. Lucky enough for us, there was a McDonald's directly across from the library and that was our first stop. He went through the drive through and ordered one strawberry milkshake without a straw or spoon. Nothing else. This was odd because my dad didn't like strawberries. He didn't like fruit of any kind. It was also strange that he wouldn't ask me if I wanted anything. None of it made sense at the time, but it would, only a few short moments later as we pulled out of the McDonald's drive through, and into the library parking lot.

It was a Sunday, so they were closed and no one was around. They clearly didn't have security cameras either because no one ever caught or said a word about what happened next. Dad proceeded to place the books in the overnight shoot, used to return books, and then promptly open the milkshake and poured it all over the books. Then, tossed the empty cup and lid in the shoot as well. Thus, all the books in the shoot got ruined, not just ours that were already destroyed. They couldn't peg it on us, and it was the perfect solution to our problem. Now, this was 1988, if something like this occurred today, you just order the book from Amazon and return that one. But back then, you had to use guerilla warfare.

★★★

As I began to think about that story from years past, it made me laugh and relax. I used that mindset and the pep talk from Camille to get through the first speech. From there, I was on my way to Sandusky, Ohio, about an hour away for the next one. On the drive to the Sandusky library it gave me a lot of time to think. I was desperate for a way to reach hundreds of people at once. I knew communication for prayers would be vital when it came to spreading the word.

The thing about social media and phone calls is, you can only reach so many people. You can put up a Facebook status or a Twitter tweet and if you're lucky only a couple hundred people will see it. But if you create a hashtag it can go viral, keeping in mind people who have never even met you can see the hashtag on someone else's feed and latch onto it. If it sounds cool, and people take their own meaning into it, it can really catch fire. I'd never created one, but it seemed obvious that something big was needed to spread the word for prayers.

You never know what you get when it comes to a book singing or a speech. I've had talks that nearly 200 people showed up to, and signings that ten people arrived at. It's a crap shoot every time, but sometimes you can strike gold even at the smallest of gatherings and this was one of those times. Only two people were waiting for me that day, but they were two great people. The Gfell family, Brooke and Jamie from Sandusky. Instead of me giving my speech, it turned into a venting session in which I told them everything that was going on with my family and they were there to listen. It was awesome to meet strangers who actually cared about, more than my sports knowledge.

We still talked a healthy dosage of sports, but we also mixed in stories about their young children. The couple was close to Emily and my age, so it was nice to relate. The wife had a huge heart and was emotional several times as we spoke. It felt great to meet new people and the support they gave was incredible. We spoke for a while and I made sure to donate a few books to the library for having me out. As I was leaving, the librarian gave me a big hug and told me, 'It sure does sound like your Mom has a lot of fight!' She was at least the fourth person to use the word 'fight' or 'fighter' when describing my mom over the last 48 hours and it was starting to stick.

As I drove from the library back home, I couldn't get the thought of a hashtag out of my head. One was needed and quickly. I pulled over at a rest stop to use the bathroom when it hit me like a ton of bricks. An idea that is, not the enchanting potpourri that is a rest stop bathroom. As I was walking, I saw this kid come out of the bathroom wearing a Kevin Owens t-shirt that said, 'Fight Owens Fight.'

Who is Kevin Owens, you might ask? He is a WWE superstar and one of my favorites' at that. People close to me know how huge of a fan of pro wrestling fan that I am. I pretty much ate, breathed and slept wrestling my whole life. Kevin Owens was a cult hero amongst 'wrasslin' fans because he wasn't the stereotypical looking pro wrestler. He was a bit chubby and not the hulking type or scary type that had dominated the wrestling scene for so many years. He was really good at cutting promos and that is why the younger generation really got behind him. He could fire up a crowd before doing a single move simply by talking and getting everyone charged up with his words. That was the sign I needed; it wouldn't be the last one either.

Just like that, 'Fight Maria Fight' was born and we were off to the races. Thank you to Kevin Owens, a small bladder and a young wrestling fan who just happened to cross my path at the exact right time! Before I could talk myself out of it, I grabbed my phone, went on Facebook and Twitter and posted a status tweet that ended with #fightmariafight. The rest is history as by the time I got home it had already been shared over 200 plus times. Then every time after that, all I had to do was pull up that hashtag, leave the next update and it was like notifying everyone at once, instead of hoping someone was going to by chance, see something online.

I'm not sure who ever thought of the concept of using a hashtag, but it was pure genius.

I wasn't home long, just long enough to grab some clean clothes, pack a snack and get ready to head back to the hospital as I knew I would once again be there all day and all night.

I knew I couldn't take time off from work to be there during the days coming up. With a new job there was just no way they were going to let that fly. It was nice enough of them to let me leave after only a few hours the previous day. I knew that once Monday rolled around, I couldn't keep doing that and hope to keep my job.

With that being the notion, I made sure to spend as much time at the hospital on the weekends as I could during the entire ordeal. I kissed the girls and Emily, grabbed my laptop and I was on my way. Secretly hoping that the next time I saw the three of them I wouldn't have to tell them the worst news possible. I grabbed my laptop because I was making it my mission to get back to everyone who was sending me messages asking for updates. The easiest way to do this was the hashtag, but I also wanted to kill time watching my mom fight. Having the laptop with me gave me the chance to not only answer people, but also document everything I was seeing. 95% of the people aware of the issues were certain she was going to die. I was certain she wasn't and I knew one day, somehow, someway, I'd be writing about this epic tale. You're reading those documented notes, aren't you? I guess grabbing the laptop and notepad paid off after all.

★★★

As I walked into the ICU waiting room it was flooded with visitors. This was an early Saturday afternoon and you would imagine people had running around to do, but nope, the place was packed. It would remain nearly 50-60 deep at all times. As word spread more and more people got behind the movement.

To me, it felt like it was filling up for two reasons. Half the people wanted to make sure they said goodbye to a person dying in a coma. They were positive she was a goner and knew that this would be their last chance to say goodbye, hoping she could somehow hear them. The other 50% of people showing up felt for the movement we had started. They, like us, just needed a damn win. They got behind the movement because somewhere in their life they lost someone suddenly. It didn't even have to be a person. It could be a job; a bad breakup, something. At one point someone or something they loved was gone and they couldn't stop it or bring it back. This was their chance to stop it from happening again. 'Fight Maria Fight' was more than a hashtag. It was a belief, a rallying call, a vision and a damn good reason to let people believe. It was their chance to right a wrong; to pull for a miracle and to rewrite the ending of a story that seemed like a forgone conclusion.

As I walked into the actual room, I saw Father Joseph Pendakar standing there. He had come to America decades earlier as a priest and known my family for 20 plus years. He had baptized some, married others and given communion to all of us at some point. He was my mothers' favorite priest and she even used to cook for him nightly when he did a stint with St. Brendan's. He was a nice man, subtle humor for someone with an extremely thick accent. He had one of those voices that would suck you in. Once you figured out what he was saying, it was usually profound and very spiritual. I used to love his homilies at mass; he just had an incredible way of speaking.

He was there upon a call from Dad to give my mom her Last Rights; this could also be known as the anointing of the sick. In the end, it pretty much means a prayer for those about to die. He said it aloud, in English as Don, Dad and I were the only ones in the room to hear it. We held hands, bowed our heads and let the words soak in. This was Saturday afternoon April 22, 2017 at around 3:30p.m.

Ten days later, Father Joe Pendakar would be in the same room, praying over the same body, but the prayer and the reason for it, would be much different...

CHAPTER SEVEN

'The human body experiences a powerful gravitational pull in the direction of hope. That is why the patient's hopes are the physician's secret weapon. They are the hidden ingredients in any prescription.'

– Norman Cousins

Hell Week

The odds were steep, we all knew that, but it wasn't going to stop me and others from believing anything was possible. You have hope as long as you tell yourself and believe there is hope. It is up to you and no one else to tell you what is and isn't possible.

As more and more people began to flood the waiting room as the day turned into a very long night, I explained my 'Fight Maria Fight' concept to a lot of people. Some got it, most snickered and thought I was nuts. One person even told me, 'face reality son, your Mom is dying.' I refused to listen. We needed a miracle and miracles happened every day. I realized the clock was ticking but it was also clicking 30 plus years ago when she laid on that table in Montreal.

★★★

As Mom fell asleep that night in Montreal, the angels in heaven were working overtime watching over her and preparing her soul for its greatest journey. The name of and destination of that journey was freedom. She had gone her whole life emotionally, physically and mentally crippled from a condition that no human being should ever have to endure.

And now, after over a quarter of a century of dealing with hell, she would have her chance to fight against the greatest villain in her life. It was a battle with the greatest prize on the line. Once again that prize was freedom. Freedom from the prison epilepsy had held her body, mind and soul captive of for so many years prior.

She was over 10,000 miles away from her bed, away from her sons, her parents and the only place she ever knew as home. She was away from those who supported her, and those who didn't support her throughout her life as well. Everything was behind her and what awaited her could be glorious if she could get there. But like a wise man once said, 'sometimes it's hell getting to heaven.' Her head was going to be cut open, not only that but it would be with a drill and a saw with no Novocain. She had a lifetime of seizures, of torment, of pissing herself, doctors, hospitals, embarrassment and never knowing when the next attack would occur. A lifetime of being scared, wondering when the hell would come back, when the pain would ever let up. Not even end, but simply give her a pain free day. For the first 99 percent of her life, it seemed as though that would never occur. Now, she was in Canada, surrounded by geniuses and about to take the chance of a lifetime. This was it, one more trip to hell for a chance at heaven.

September 23, 1983 had arrived. The nurses came in bright and early and scooped Mom up out of bed. They brought her down to the special bathtub rinsing her down with the special solution. They dried her off, put the gown back on and brought her back up to the room where

Dad was waiting for her. He had a gown on over his clothes so he was able to hug her. It was less than an hour until surgery and Mom was ready.

Dr. Feindel walked into the room and introduced himself to Dad. It was the first time they had met. Dr. Feindel explained that if they could not cure the epilepsy with the surgery without causing serious damage to other parts of Mom, then he wouldn't do it. He told them that he would not take away one illness just to give the patient nine new ones. He explained that if he was going to remove a piece of her brain with scar tissue on it, that he would only do it if it wasn't a part she needed to see, hear, feel, walk, or any other vital function. He was going in her brain for one reason, to remove tissue and stop seizures, if it wasn't possible, then he would stop the surgery. He was not willing to take risks to make things worse for her.

Mom and Dad were in agreement with the doctor. Mom then turned and reached for the holy water. In this jug was holy water from every shrine the blessed Mother Mary had appeared at in Fatima. It was also mixed in with 12 ounces of holy water blessed by Pope John Paul II. Mom informed Dr. Feindel that she needed to bless him with the holy water before she would allow him to perform the surgery on her. Dr. Feindel agreed and bent down so Mom could bless his forehead. She also blessed his hands, and feet as she knew he would be on them up to 12 hours during the operation. She then blessed Dad with it, and had him bless her with it as well.

Dr. Feindel suggested that the rest of the water come into surgery with them.

Not only would the holy water be brought in, but it would be poured on Mom at certain parts of the surgery as she prayed. Dr. Feindel knew that it was key to keep Mom calm during the surgery, and this would help. He was a great man to allow such an intense request.

As the moving bed rolled down the hall to the operating room, and Mom inched closer to the surgery that would hopefully save her life and make it worth living, Dad was right by her side holding her hands. The other patients were also standing there wishing her well. She said her goodbye to Dad as they wheeled her in and she told him she loved him one last time. The moment of truth had arrived.

The procedure started with numerous doctors entering the room and getting everything prepped. Mom had her entire body strapped down, unable to move in any way. Her head was positioned inside of a small metal cage and the nurse rubbed a cold cream all over her bald skull to prep it for surgery. The sawing began and Mom was in intense pain but she knew all the screaming in the world wouldn't make it stop and she also knew this is what needed to happen. The doctors took turns, drilling and cutting for what seemed liked hours. As the intense pain of the drilling was filling her body, she tried to focus on the man in front of her who was repeating the Our Father over and over. She just kept repeating Jesus' name as the sickening feeling and sound of the drill split her head wide open.

It was the worst pain she had ever felt in her life. They needed to drill three holes total, in the shape of a triangle. Once the first whole was drilled into her skull, they inserted a sharp wire that went under the skull cap and through the other two holes as well underneath the skull cap so they didn't have to touch the brain. When all the drilling, stretching and sawing was done, her brain was swollen, but ready for the rest of the surgery to take place. Her brain was totally exposed and she could see it through the mirror on the ceiling.

Unfortunately, the drilling wasn't done just yet, they still had to drill ten more holes in her skull. These would be the holes they would need to use later on to insert and pin the skull cap back on with nickel pins.

The worst part of the surgery was over and now it was time for Dr. Feindel to take over. They began with what is called "mapping the brain," this is done to see what part of the patient's body was controlled by each part of the brain they would be working with. They would insert a fine wire into the brain and then when they would touch that neuron with it, a part of the body would react.

It didn't take long for the doctors to realize her brain was far from normal. When they touched a nerve that should have caused her to urinate, instead it made her right pinky move. When they touched a part of her brain that should have made her cry, instead it made her wink. It was very clear early into the surgery that they were going to have numerous issues to contend with. The neuro testing went on for the next six hours as they were hoping to find the scarred neuron that was causing her to have seizures and attempt to fix it. After they had roughly 366 wires through her entire brain without finding the one scarred neuron causing the seizures, the doctor was ready to throw in the towel.

Mom blacked out and a miracle would occur. Mom said that God came to her and delivered to her a message that she had been through enough pain and that it was over now. Mom says she saw the faces of all of her dead relatives and had a real look into heaven, before realizing it was not her time.

When she opened up her eyes Dr. Fiendel explained to her that she had gone into a grand mal seizure. Her heart and all functioning organs had stopped and it appeared she had died on the table. When she came out of the seizure, and her body kicked back in Dr. Feindel was able to find the scar tissue causing the seizures. They would spend the next four hours fixing them. After ten hours, the surgery was close to being done and Dr. Feindel left the operating room as the last doctor would focus on putting Mom's skull back together with 12 nickel pins and sowed the cap back together.

Dr. Fiendel then brought Dad into the room to see his wife after 10 plus hours of waiting and worrying. She spent the next two hours with Dad and Dr. Fiendel talking about the surgery and everything that happened during it. Her brain was already working properly, only hours after the surgery and Dad picked up the phone and called home so his wife could hear the sounds and voices of those she loved. After speaking with her parents, siblings and son, she hung up and began to rest. Dad fixed the blankets around her and sat with her until she fell asleep. He had to leave the next day because of the arrangements that were made.

By the third day post-surgery, she was able to walk on her own, and even go to the library at the school and read. She took great enjoyment in sitting on the balcony of the hospital and looking over to the soccer / football field at McGill University to watch the rugby games taking place.

Over the following three weeks, Mom would be put through every test that was given to her before surgery to see how her brain improved. It was vital to see if the tests showed improvement and to make sure nothing got worse. She hadn't had any issues, no seizures, no shocks, not even a jolt. She just kept getting stronger each day. If she could make it until October 28 without having any seizures or major issues, the institute would release her to go home. As the days went on, she got better and stronger. Mom already had visions and plans for even the simplest of pleasure for when she returned home. It truly was a miracle.

★★★

Again, I fully realize all of that was 30 plus years ago. But knowing that story gave me tremendous faith that miracles *do* happen. If one miracle per life can happen, why not two? *Let's go for it* was my motto as I kept thinking there would be plenty of time to cry and be sad if things went bad, but for now, why not go for it.

As Saturday evening turned into Sunday, it was more of the same. A long chain of people coming in and out and praying over Mom. It was weird in a way because a lot of people were saying goodbye as if this was a wake. It was one of the few times a hospital visit seemed like a full-blown wake. Her room even became flooded with pictures, which was actually really nice. It just couldn't have flowers because, allegedly, flowers can suck oxygen out of the room. Something that would go on to be a great debate as people actually began to argue with each other over flowers and oxygen. I didn't care, I feel as though when people are deeply sad or frightened, they look for anything to take their attention off it for a bit. If debating over flowers was going to make people feel better, I had no issues with it. I personally didn't care to be quite honest about it.

Social media aside, that Sunday was also the day I started hearing from older people who didn't have it. Not only the people who went to my home church of St. Brendan's, but also other neighboring churches such as St. Angela, St. Richards, St. Clarence, St. Patrick's etc. Apparently, Mom's name was placed on a prayers chain throughout the Catholic Dioceses and everyone from St. Bernadette to St. Ambrose seemed to know about and be praying for my Mom.

The rest of the day went pretty smoothly with people in and out and little to no aggravation. This was nice for Dad as that would be the last thing he needed. I also had Emily bring up the girls as this was the longest Dad had gone without seeing them since either one was born. Even on days in which my parents didn't watch them, he would find a reason to stop over a few extra times a week to see them. Sometimes he would have candy or a toy with him as well. We could tell he was missing the girls and needed to see them. With the way the ICU works, the girls couldn't visit Mom, but they could wait in the waiting room as Dad came out to see them. His face instantly lit up and it was the best emotional medicine for him. In fact, I think it finally relaxed him a bit as that was the first night he went home since Mom was on the vent.

After everyone left, I stuck around and wrote. People smoke, they drink, they have sex, they do a lot of things to relax and get away from stressful issues. I write! It is my escape, my passion, my desire and my mistress. Focus sets in, pain goes away and it is one of the greatest escapes I can give myself. It's an addiction, it really is, my mind is constantly moving, creating, escaping! I had brought my laptop that day and kept in a bag, waiting for inspiration to peak. As the evening turned into late night, it was time to create. The crazy thing is, looking back at it now, I can't tell you what I wrote about. I have a photographic memory of just about everything, but on this one, I simply don't remember. It didn't matter, again, it was an escape.

Monday morning rolled around yet again, and it was much of the same. Checking my phone once every 5-10 minutes at work, waiting on word about Mom. Thank God for Don being there, allowing me to work and get my mind off of things for a few minutes each day. Also thank God for Carrie Pell who once again stepped up and chipped in to help watch the girls. She took Monday and Tuesday mornings over, while Mandi, a friend of ours from church took the afternoons on those two days. Mandi and Carrie were gifts from heaven to say the least. They really helped out and gave us one less thing to worry about. The girls took to them both and it was a perfect match.

Monday came and went with nothing of too much significance happening until the very end of the night. Right before I left, the doctor pulled Dad and I back into a meeting with just him. He said that Mom was showing small signs of improvement, but nothing that would lead him to believe she was going to make it. He went on to explain that he could take the vent down from 95% to around 75% which was a sizable jump. He said that would more than likely be the best it would ever get and it would also cause her eyes to pop open and roll around. He explained the eyes rolling would give people false hope and that I needed to explain to family and friends that fact as well. I told Dad not to say anything. I was fine with giving people a little false hope. I figured that may be all they get.

Tuesday was another day of the same, but as the doctor warned as people came in one after another visiting, they saw the eyes rolling to the response of the body fighting harder for that oxygen and it gave them hope. I didn't have the heart to tell them any different. For all they knew, she was getting better and that is what I wanted them to think. The eye rolling was also a fact of less morphine being pumped in her as well. More so the less morphine than the less oxygen was the true reason. Whatever the case may be, it gave people hope and I sure as hell wasn't going to say anything.

The only person who really knew what was going on was one of Mom's best friends,

Cathy Wade. She was so smart and also a two-time cancer survivor. She knew her stuff, and not only was she very sweet but also extremely intelligent. She asked the doctor if Mom was on less morphine right away, and of course, a doctor can't lie. So, there it was. Even if she didn't ask the doctor, I would have cracked and told her. Cathy was amazing and not the kind of woman you kept anything from. She was always understanding and never judging of me or others. She was so honest, so open and so caring. She was one of the most selfless people I have ever met and her and I became very close.

In fact, I wrote a book in 2016 that featured an entire chapter about her cancer battles. Cathy came into my life in my junior year of high school as I was in choir with her daughter, Katie. She was just so nice to me from day one, and always treated me like a son, that I couldn't help but love her like she was an aunt. She tragically got cancer again and passed away in July of 2019. It was one of the hardest things I have ever dealt with on a personal level. I think about her every day and miss her. She will never get to hold a grandchild, or go to another concert in the park with her husband, but her spirit will always be felt. I miss her terribly.

On that night, talking with Cathy was my solace. Like it was many nights. She was a straight shooter, never lied or messed around. What you saw was what you got and I think that's why we clicked so much. I knew I could confide in her on how I truly felt about things. I confessed to her that even though I was "rah rah" on the outside and tried rallying the troops, on the inside I had little to no hope. I explained that my mom was only human, and even a cat would only have nine lives. We both laughed at the cat comment. We both wanted Mom to live, clearly, but I think we both knew that we had to face the reality head on, if the worst did happen and she never got better.

Another day turned into night, which turned into morning with little to no progress. Mom struggled through the night and by Wednesday morning, the vent was turned back to 90%. It had been nearly a week on this thing with little to no movement. A gut punch for sure. Like a hot knife through a big stick of soft butter. ARDS was running right through Mom and it looked worse by the day. One good thing about Wednesday was that I had a slight reprieve from going straight to the hospital from work. Maggie had soccer practice and I a good reason to focus on something else for a few hours.

Maggie was so sweet, so innocent and didn't quite understand the serious situation we were all facing. Watching her play soccer that evening was a great escape. A good enough reason to forget the personal hell going on, and reflect on the blessings in our life. Meanwhile baby Zook Zook was as happy as can be slugging down a bottle and laying back in her onesie.

I did mention to Emily that we would need to start breaking the news to Maggie soon enough however, that just in case this one didn't have a happy ending we would need to prepare her. This would be tough as Maggie often referred to Mom as her, 'Number One Gal!'

As we drove home after practice with Maggie, we tried to explain a little bit further as to what was going on with her 'Mage Kee' as she called Mom. As smart as Maggie was, it didn't take much to explain things to her. Clearly, we couldn't get into any graphic details, but I think we drove the point home as best we could. Maggie was sad, but like any child full of hope and spirit. With the Fight Maria Fight movement gaining steam by the second, I took a picture of Maggie in her soccer uniform and posted it on the hashtag, with the request for prayers. It continued to go viral and I firmly believe it gave people something to root for.

Even if you didn't like Mom, or me or whatever, it didn't matter. That picture of Maggie in the uniform gave soccer moms and grandmas everywhere a reason to pray. I realize it may sound silly to some, but it is not. Sometimes, all it takes is one thing to relate to that can give anyone a chance to pray or believe in a greater cause.

When I eventually got to the ICU that night, I could tell quickly that Dad was worn down. He looked exhausted, depressed and left with little to no hope. It was one of those nights sitting with him that very little was said. Normally, no matter the situation my Dad and I were never short on words and could make each other laugh, but that night was not to be. Reality was now setting in more than ever and as Mom showed little to no improvement at all, the clock was ticking loudly.

As I left, I hugged my Dad and said, 'remember boy, sometimes the sky is darkest right before sunrise.' A silly cliché, but one that is very true. I felt as though we couldn't drop any lower, and as bad as it seemed, we could have been heading for that miracle after all. Dad responded that he was getting fed up with the constant bad news, and just wanted to be told something positive. Secretly, I felt the same way and wanted the same thing.

Another day came and went with no progress, and the hourglass was just about out of sand.

Thursday rolled around, and it was clear that we needed a distraction; anything would do but the fact that the NFL draft was the next day was almost like a sign from God. It was as if he was sending a small gift for one night at least. In Cleveland, the NFL draft is like the damn Superbowl for many. It's the night of year when the worst franchise in sports has a little hope that things may turn around.

As the Browns selected Myles Garrett with the number one overall pick, I told my Dad that if the Browns could finally get some good news, then maybe we were in store for some as well. I said that the Garrett selection was a sign that maybe the Browns were finally turning things around and that maybe we were now in store for our sign that things may turn around for our family too. The Browns would go 0-16 the following season after going 1-15 the prior season. Yes, they found a way to get worse.

It was a silly analogy. I was looking for any reason possible to encourage everyone to keep praying and hoping that we were headed for a miracle. We just needed one sign, one ray of hope, something, we needed something. The next morning, I would get that sign as it came in tenfold and the first indication that "Hell Week" may finally be turning around.

CHAPTER EIGHT

'We want big directional signs from God. God just wants us to pay attention.' – Lysa TerKeurst

Signs

Friday April 28, 2018 will go down as a day I will never forget as it was the first during the entire saga that gave me real hope. It was one of those days where science was telling us one thing, but faith was telling us another. I chose faith as it was the only one that kept me and others from giving up.

The numbers were still bad, Mom improved slightly throughout the night and the machine was now down to 80%, meaning she was doing 20% of the breathing on her own. However, despite the slight improvement the clock was still ticking and time was absolutely running out.

I was off work that day and headed straight to the hospital. By the grace of God my job was closed that particular day as it was a pre-determined floating holiday given to us. It couldn't have come at a more perfect time. A random floating holiday on a day in which I needed it the most. Perhaps the first sign in a weekend of them.

It had been nine days since Mom was placed on the vent, and seven days since the big 'live or die meeting' held at the hospital. I then called my Dad and told him to stay home and get some rest that morning. I let him know I had it handled and would sit with Mom until he was ready to come in. He needed a few hours to breathe and I was more than happy to have some solitude as well.

I got there bright and early and that is the best time to be at the ICU. It's calm, few people are there and everyone is sleeping. It can be peaceful at times as you just hear the beeps of the machines, the scratching of pens on a clipboard from doctors, and the sound of hope in the air. It could have been despair in the air as well, but I kept choosing to ignore that. There would be plenty of time to be sad later.

I took the alone time with Mom to talk to her. Sure, she couldn't talk back, but it didn't stop me. I talked her head off for at least an hour straight. I read her some prayers, I told her some inspirational stories. I even went as far to requote inspirational movie parts I had heard and memorized from movies like *Rocky, Miracle, Any Given Sunday* and various others. I took the urns from my parents' house that were now in her room of my late Uncle Pete and Aunt Josephine. I placed them next to her head and started yelling at her to use their strength to come back to us. I tried everything. After over an hour of talking to her, I just slumped down in the chair and began to pray. I got totally lost in the moment until I felt a hand on my shoulder. I looked up and it was this man I had never seen before in my life. Well, at least, not that I could remember, but he sure knew who I was.

He said, 'Vincent, don't you remember me?' I knew right there that it had to be family related because only family members ever called me Vincent. The man turned out to be Father Bob Lindquist from St. Patrick's in West

Park. To say he knew me would be an understatement, he was the first priest to ever hold me as he was the one who baptized me.

I hadn't seen him in 35 years as he stopped his priesthood and became a family man. He was super nice and sat there and prayed with me. He told me everything would be okay as he had a special prayer he was going to say. Again, I must stress this, he was genuinely a nice man. Sometimes people can try to pull off being nice and genuine, but if they are not it will show through. This man was 100% legitimate. It was great to see him and the fact that he knew me and knew my mom was there was a clear sign someone had gotten hold of him. He stayed for about an hour and it was a very nice visit. It was random but pretty darn neat to meet the man who baptized me after all these years.

A random day off, Father Lindquist showing up, things were starting to look up. We were a quick two for two to start the day.

Moments after he left Don and Dad both showed up. I noticed right away they both had haircuts. I asked them why and they explained that the chance of us having a wake and funeral was strong, so the haircut may be needed for all of us. The haircut measure was a pretty cold dose of reality as it began to sink in further. They made a lot of sense; we had seen over 200 people in just over a week. The wake and funeral would be sure to bring about five times that many people to it, so we'd owed it to Mom to look our best. I stayed a little longer and then left to get a haircut of my own.

The random day off when I needed one badly and the surprise appearance of Father Lindquist may have been tiny signs. Perhaps even small coincidences, but what happened next was the clearest of all signs that something was in the air. I pulled into Lady Jane's in North Olmsted and sat in the lobby for a bit. It was semi crowded for a Friday afternoon when most people should have been at work. I took the time to respond to as many people as I could as the constant instant messages were nonstop. Finally, my name was called from the receptionist and it was my turn for the chair.

I like Lady Jane's because the women who cut your hair are nice and *most of them* do a good job. I stress 'most of them' because every once and in a while you may just get chopped! But at only $16 a cut, it is worth the risk and I plopped myself in the seat looking not to say a word. Sometimes you get lucky and the barber, oh I'm sorry, 'stylist' will not force much small talk. Sometimes, you get Chatty Cathy. You never quite know which way it is going to go. On this day for obvious reasons, I wasn't in the talkative mood, but that would change quickly. The woman who was about to cut my hair looked really sad. She was this beautiful woman about my age of Latin descent. I was taken back not only by her beauty but by this incredibly sad look on her face that almost had me in tears.

I debated for a few minutes if I should say something, and after a while I finally couldn't take it and asked her what the matter was. She instantly stopped the haircut and opened up to me. She explained how her mother Maria was in the Fairview ICU with a brain injury.

I about choked when I heard her say that, so I asked if everything was going to be okay? She went on to explain to me that her mother was epileptic and incurred her brain injury during a recent seizure. I was floored. I mean absolutely stunned with what I was hearing. What happened next took the cake however.

I asked her to stop with the haircut, hold my hand and pray with me. I didn't inform her of my own personal hell going on, also with an epileptic mother named Maria. Rather I just let her know that I was there for her, and we needed to pray. The fact that we both had epileptic mothers, named Maria, in the Fairview ICU was just too much of a sign to ignore. I grabbed her hand and said a few words. It was then she asked me if we could say the Hail Mary together because it was her Mom's favorite prayer. Mom's favorite prayer was also the Hail Mary as Mom was a gigantic Mother Mary follower. Mom had gone on countless retreats and been a part of countless prayer groups to honor Mary. In fact, I didn't know a single soul who loved Mary as much as she did.

The teaching of Mary was so important in our family that the statue had to be prominently displayed in our house and also at my brother's and my wedding. Mother Mary was a big deal in the McKee home, a very big deal. When friends of mine who were married were trying to get pregnant, Mom would give them prayer cards and pray to Mary with them.

For years and years my Christmas and birthday gifts to my Mom were always Mary related. If you could picture some weird old lady with a bunch of troll dolls at a bingo hall for good luck, then you can picture walking into my Mom's living room which was more or less a shrine to the Blessed Mother. Unlike the troll dolls, there was nothing weird about this. It was quite moving actually and her dedication to Mary inspired me many a time. I personally thought it was absolutely beautiful and have had Mother Mary appear in several of my dreams over the years. Another big thing with the Hail Mary is its large presence in the rosary. My mom had rosaries draped everywhere and

I myself have carried one in my pocket since I was a little boy.

Mom and I butted heads a lot, but the one thing I could never argue with her about was her faith: it was strong! It was also a huge reason that I was not giving up and not allowing anyone else to give up either.

If the name, the Fairview ICU and the Hail Mary weren't enough, what I saw next put it over the top for good. The stylist who never told me her name, so we'll just keep calling her stylist, removed her smock to hug me. I noticed a large tattoo on her right arm, and a small tattoo on the left. The right arm had a tattoo of the Chinese symbol for peace. It wouldn't have been a big thing if I didn't have the exact same one on my right arm in the exact spot. But that wasn't even the topper. Oh no, she proceeds to turn around in which I got a clear shot at the massive tattoo on her left arm of a praying statue of Mary with the rosary hanging from her hands. The exact same statue I had bought my Mom once for her birthday.

That was it, case closed, filed to the court. Mom was living! You couldn't tell me any different. I had never seen this stylist before or after, and when I went back months later and asked for her, they told me no one of Latin descent with that description had ever even worked there. Was she an angel? Was it a sign? My God I don't know, but I think about it often and smile.

The second I got back in my car, before even reaching for my keys to place them in the ignition, I sent out a mass text to all my relatives that I could think of in that brief moment guaranteeing a miracle was on the way. The tattoo of Mother Mary sealed the deal for me. It truly did. Every time I closed my eyes the next few days all I could see was that tattoo, the statue of Mary I bought my mom with the same pose and my Mom laying there on the vent gasping for life. Those same three images over and over again.

When I finally did compose myself and start the car, I noticed a shiny red signal was no longer blinking. My check engine light which had been on for the last several months was now gone. Being so new into a job, having very little time and quite frankly worried about it being something that would cost a lot of money, I just never got it checked. It became quite the sore subject between Emily and I at times too, but suddenly it was gone. I couldn't believe it so I drove up the street to Auto Zone and had the guy check the computer system. He said, 'Sir your car is doing just fine, despite having over 120,000 miles on it, it still has plenty of fight.' He used that exact wording, 'plenty of fight.'

Interesting choice of words to say the least, but again, at this point I may have been grasping at straws. I hadn't eaten in days and didn't have to pick up the girls for a few more minutes so I couldn't resist stopping through a drive through. The multitude of good signs that morning allowed me the adrenaline and excitement to have an appetite again. I swung across the street and picked up some grub via the drive through. After placing my order, I couldn't help but notice the vanity plate of the car in front of me. Clear as day it read, 'FITEMLM'.

Now I'll be honest, I do not remember the make or model of the car. I don't remember what state it was from but I sure as hell remember that license plate. For those of you wondering the importance of 'MLM', my Mom's middle name is Lina. So, her initials are MLM.

I sat there stunned until a loud horn woke me up from the guy in the line behind me. I looked in the mirror and waved. I then pulled up still trying to compute in my head what I had just seen. The guy in the window handed me my bag of grease and salt, I mean, my lunch, and when I asked him how much I owed him, he said nothing.

'Huh?' It was all I could muster as I wasn't sure what was going on. The young man then explained that the woman in the car in front of me paid my bill. When I asked why he said, 'She said you looked like you could use it.' Okay then, I grabbed my straw and was on my way.

From Father Lindquist and a stylist with a tattoo, to a check engine light and license plate with my mom's initials, something was in the air that fateful Friday. I'm not sure if the food tasted so good because it was free, or paid for by perhaps a guardian angel. Sign or coincidence? Time would tell.

The rest of the day went smoothly and I would head back up to the hospital with the girls for a bit until Emily could meet me up there and take them back home. Bringing the girls to my Dad truly was the best medicine for him at that point. Certain people who will remain nameless gave me a lot of shit for bringing Madelyn who was only nine months old into the hospital. But quite frankly, unless you're going to volunteer to watch her so my wife and I can be at the hospital together with my parents, then please just shut the hell up. And yes, that was my exact stance at that point and is to this day.

The rest of the day went pretty smoothly despite no improvement shown by Mom. I told everyone I saw that evening about the tattoo and the license plate. Some people saw it as hope, others thought I was grasping at straws. Maybe it was a little of both, time would answer that question soon enough.

Driving home about 2a.m., I took the long way back. Instead of the direct route down Lorain Road though Fairview, I drove backwards towards Cleveland Hopkins Airport. It is where I grew up; it is also where my Grandparents lived on Forestwood for 30 plus years. It was also where my brother Donald and I grew up on Midvale which was just one street over from Grandparents' all those years. It has since all gone; the Airport bought all that land in the late 90s, levelling the house in the process. It was also within seconds of the Projects Section 8 housing, so a long visit on this night was out of the cards. However, nothing was going to stop me from getting out of the car and walking around for a little bit at least. Nothing could be any scarier than what we were all going through at that point anyway.

So, I did just that. Parked my car on the side of the street and just started walking around. A lot of it is blocked off but some of it isn't if you're willing to climb through some dirt and hop a few fences. I closed my eyes and thought back to a happier time. A time when my Uncle

Pete and Aunt Jo were still around. A time without pain, a time with innocence and unbridled hope. A simpler time, no doubt, but one that will never go away in my heart or my head.

It was where I learned how to ride a bike, hit a baseball, read a book, and where my love of sports began. It was where my family celebrated so many holidays. So many weddings and newborn babies. So many tears of both happiness and joy. I looked down at my arm and it was trembling, not from fear, not from the thick cold April air, but from hope! The hair on the back of my neck stood up, and even with the chill in the air, I was dripping in sweat from the moment I was experiencing. I bent down and dug at the soil. When we moved from Midvale to North Olmsted in 1990, my Dad buried a time capsule with a keepsake from all of us in it. I had no idea if I was standing in our old backyard or not. Again, how the hell could I tell? Everything was gone and replaced with baseball field and just fields of dirt.

After a few minutes I realized the chances of finding that capsule were slim to none so I decided to take the moment in a different direction. I grabbed some of the dirt and put it in my pocket. I then drove back to the ICU and went in my Mom's room; it was well past 3a.m. and no one was around. I proceeded to take the dirt from pocket and rub it all over her feet and then put the socks they had back on her. I left right away so no one would walk by and wonder what the hell I was doing.

Call me crazy and I wouldn't blame you, but I just thought if she had the soil on her from which I was born on, it may change the outcome. I had that same thought process running through my head about 20 minutes later when I pulled into St. Bernadette's parking lot. A church about two minutes from my house in Westlake, Ohio. I went up to the statue of Mary they have and rubbed some of the remaining soil I had with me on her feet as well. I'm pretty sure I shouldn't have been doing that and could have gotten in serious trouble if caught. But at close to 4a.m., desperation and lack of sleep take over your decision making.

★★★

Saturday morning came with the alarm clock not even going off. If it did, I was in a dead sleep and never heard it. By the time I rolled over and looked at the clock, it was well past 10a.m. and my wake-up call came via a little bean named Maggie McKee pouncing on me. There is no better feeling! I snuggled up with Maggie for what felt like an eternity. She asked me to read her a book. I said sure and one book turned into ten. It was such a nice feeling that I didn't care how many books she wanted me to read, I wasn't getting out of that bed until I absolutely had to.

As nice as it was, I eventually had to get up and get the day moving. Like any stressful situation it doesn't take much for a stupid argument to break out and sure enough Emily and I had one. She had been extremely supportive of everything going on and I couldn't thank her enough. Even before this, as a sportswriter on top of actual 8a.m. to 5p.m. job, I was gone 15 straight Friday nights every fall covering high school football. She put up with a lot so I could chase my dream and I couldn't thank her enough for doing so. This was different however as the source of grief was my going to the hospital so much without her.

She had a point, but I had zero tolerance for anything upsetting so of course it led to a stupid argument that seemed to go on for an hour. Her main point of contention was that I was spending so much time at the hospital and not taking her. As I said earlier, we were using all of our babysitting help during the week and I wasn't going to ask those people to put in overtime at no pay. And again, certain people were giving me crap for taking the girls to the hospital when I did.

Emily's point was that she wanted time at the hospital with me there so we can visit and talk to people and just feel better. She didn't want the girls there because then she couldn't focus. To her point, looking at it now, I understand. At the time, I was furious and stormed out.

I just, I had had enough and wasn't in the mood for anything. I got in the car and drove, but not far. For whatever reason I didn't know where to go. I didn't care. I just had to leave and not be there. I went from 0mph to 60mph of being happy with Maggie to angry with Emily. I needed out!

I ended up at a local bowling alley of all places. It was close. I was pissed and I just needed to go to a place no one could find me. A bowling alley seemed perfect and it was. The crazy things you do when you're stressed out of your mind. I don't bowl or care to learn, but that is where I ended up regardless. I wasn't there to bowl, or cheer on anyone bowling, I was just there. It made no sense but for whatever the reason it made me feel better. As I sat there with a burger and a soda, I just felt better. It didn't matter if it was Big Earn McCracken, Roy Munson or DJ Jobber Joe in front of me, it was a distraction.

Whomever it was, however, did grab my attention and had me cheering for him soon enough. As I looked up, this guy was tossing a perfect game seven frames in. Two more strikes later and this man was on the cusp of perfection. It was pretty cool to watch as I had never seen one in person and I found myself pulling for this guy pretty hard. After he hit his 12th straight strike (you have to hit 3 straight in the 10th frame), him and his pals started going berserk in celebration. It was really cool and as he was jumping up and down. Something went flying out of his pocket and right towards where was sitting. After a few moments of wondering if I should grab it for him, I bent down to pick it up and sure enough, it was a rosary.

I picked it up and walked over to give it to him but he already started his next game and didn't want to be bugged. His buddy told me to keep it and get the heck away from them. Bowlers.

So, I did just that, putting it in my pocket and walking away. I grabbed my burger, my soda and nacho's, I had gone back and ordered more food. My appetite was finally back and I was smashing some excellent bowling alley bar food. As I walked back into the bar area and sat down, my phone was buzzing once again. This time it was not someone asking for an update but rather my Dad calling to scold me.

Apparently, Emily called him to vent her frustration with my storming off and Dad gave me what for. I had no chance. I had to go home. Before I could pay my growing tab, grab my keys and go home, I noticed my phone was going off yet again. This time it was my Aunt Anna who lived with my grandparents to take care of them. She was recently divorced and it was the perfect fit for her to live there and watch after them. Her car was down and she wanted to go with me to visit Mom. This was actually perfect timing as I we spoke and I let her know how pissed Emily was. So, Anna told me that she would watch the kids that night so Emily and I could visit and then get dinner somewhere and be alone for a few seconds to get our minds off everything. It was the perfect solution to a growing problem.

The plan was set, swing home and pick up the girls, all three of them, then head to my grandparents to pick up Anna. It worked out perfectly as several of my cousins were there to sit with the girls while Emily, Anna and I went to visit Mom.

It was a nice visit and we were there several hours before heading back to Parma Heights to drop Anna off with the girls. By this point, my cousin Annamarie and my aunt Franny were at my Grandparents as well. It was nice to see everyone and both girls seemed completely fine so Emily and I left to get some dinner. We decided to meet up with my friends Joe and Karen at a local sports bar in North Olmsted. I didn't even care the insane miles getting put on the car that day going back and forth from North Olmsted to Parma, to Fairview, back to Parma, back to North Olmsted and eventually back to Parma later that night, only to finish the night going from Parma back home. It was just nice to get out and relax for a few minutes.

As we sat there with Joe and Karen they told us about all the memories that they had shared with my Mom over the years. I had known Joe since third grade, and Karen since high school. In fact, before I got my first car late into my senior year, Karen used to drive me home from school. They were a good couple of friends and pretty much the only married couple we hung around with.

My mom loved them both dearly as she had done Karen's hair several times in high school and Joe had been coming around our family for nearly 20 years. Hanging with Joe and Karen that night brought the perfect distraction with things in my life becoming so serious. Joe and I could laugh about anything and make it funny. Sometimes I would make him laugh so hard it would give him the hiccups. Again, it was the exact medicine we all needed on such a serious night. It was also a nice reminder that life was still going on around me even if it seemed as though my life was stuck in a bubble of gloom and doom.

In the middle of the laughing and joking I got a phone call from a number I didn't recognize. I thought for sure another one of my Mom or Dad's friends had tracked down my number and wanted an update. I was happy to take the call and excused myself from the bar and headed outside. Except, it wasn't a call about my mom, it was a call that would forever change my life.

Calling me at that moment was Terry Lawriw, CEO and Owner of the AFC Cleveland Royals. The defending National Premier Soccer League (NPSL) National Champions. They were an outdoor soccer franchise and a championship team in need of a broadcaster for their championship defense season. Terry had seen some of my work covering indoor soccer over the years with the Cleveland Freeze and Cleveland Legacy, and also read my book Cleveland's Finest. That is the only book out there that highlights the championship runs of the Cleveland Crunch in the mid to late 1990s. Before I could even realize it, my name was starting to become aligned with Cleveland soccer, and I absolutely loved it! As the years went on, my name would get even bigger, but when you're focused on nothing but fulfilling your passion and being your best, name value never motivates me. I simply wanted to be my best and leave nothing on the table.

He was calling to tell me that because of my knowledge covering soccer, and several radio interviews he heard me give, he thought I would be the perfect man for the job. This was one of the greatest phone calls I had ever taken as I almost stood there in shock with what I was hearing. I gladly accepted the position on the announce team and thanked him profusely for the faith in me. He went on to explain that they were having a practice the next day at 6p.m. at Independence High School. It was a perfect chance for me to come and meet the team along with the coaching staff. I quickly said yes and thanked him again before ending the call and heading back inside to give everyone the great news.

It had been two plus weeks of sadness and heartache, two plus weeks of one bad news item after another. It was glorious to get this one thing that I had been dreaming about my entire life. Until this point, I had only been known as a writer and there was nothing wrong with that, but my dream since as far back as I could remember was to call sports. I had worked so hard for it for so many years and it was finally happening. To this day I don't know if the two things are related, maybe God knew it was my time. I truly don't know, but it couldn't have happened at a better time. The only shame of it all was that I couldn't pick up the phone and call my parents who I so badly wanted to share the news with.

I did know that it was another sign in a 24-hour time period packed with good ones. I couldn't reason it. I couldn't patch them all together, but I just knew something was going on. God was telling me something. He was trying to tip me off that even if the worst was to come, a bright future awaited in some form. I just didn't know it yet.

That night was also symbolic as it is the night my daughter Madelyn got her nickname of 'Zookie', which would also be known as 'The Zook' and 'Baby Zook Zook.' Apparently while we were out, my cousin Annie, Grandma, Aunt Franny and Aunt Anna had a hard time quelling one of her crying spells. Sometimes Zook would have a hard time settling down, as most 9-month old's would when a crying jag started and their mother was not around to soothe them. After 30 plus minutes of screaming and crying, they resorted to making funny noises and sounds, one of which was 'Zookie Zookie Zoo.' For whatever reason, it was the only thing that calmed her down. So, they just kept on doing it until she fell asleep.

To this very day we call her 'Zook' and the story lives in infamy. If I call her Madelyn, sometimes she doesn't even respond, but if I call her 'Zook,' she answers right away. In perhaps what was one of the craziest 48-hour stretches of my life, as Mom laid on her death bed, this one moment produced smiles that have lasted ever since. There is light in any darkness, and 'The Zook' brought us just that!

After I made sure both girls were sound asleep in their bed, and Emily was crashed out in our bed, I left one more time. This time back to Fairview and the ICU I went. I wanted to tell Mom about the announcing position, it was too big not to take and if the unthinkable happened, I wanted to tell her while she was still alive.

Depending on what book you read, or what expert you listen to, they say that a patient can hear you while they are in the medicated coma. I've spoken with patients who said they could, and others who will tell you they couldn't remember a thing. Regardless, I was telling Mom the good news. It's kind of odd telling someone who can't respond. You almost fool yourself into thinking the news may shock them into responding, but for me it just felt good to tell her. Both my parents were so supportive of my work that I felt this break was every bit as much for them as it was for me. I gave her a kiss on the forehead and headed home once and for all.

A day that started off with sleeping in and cuddling with my Bean, ended with more miles put on my car then I could have imagined, but every one of them well worth it. From North Olmsted to Parma, to Fairview, back to Parma, back to North Olmsted, back to Parma, back to North Olmsted, back to Fairview, back to North Olmsted to bed. A lot of driving, a lot of thinking, a lot of healing.

★★★

April 30th, 2017 was our last attempt to get everyone together and throw a Hail Mary, both figuratively and literally. As many members of our family as possible gathered at the church and said The Rosary in the Chapel area of Fairview Church. My best friend Dave Murphy came as well and that meant a lot.

At this point it looked like the end was near so Abbie was driving in with Matthew my nephew to say goodbye as well. As they were on the road from North Carolina, we put her on speaker phone as she was driving so Matt and her could pray with us as well. It was truly all hands-on deck at such a pivotal time.

Mom had checked into the hospital on Tuesday April 18th, went on the vent the early hours of Thursday April 20th. It was clear, time was running out. After we prayed, we all headed back upstairs to the ICU for some more visiting time. I couldn't stick around as I had to go to the soccer practice and meet everyone in person. I wanted to stick around but at the same time, knew that a distraction was needed, especially one of this magnitude.

I also knew I would stop back at some point that night.

My Dad's cousin, Sarah, is as close to an angel on this Earth as they come. I had met Cousin Sarah a few years prior and have grown close with her ever since. She is more than a distant relative, she is a friend, and someone who I trust with some of my deepest thoughts and feelings. Even though she is technically a cousin, I often look at her as an Aunt. I trusted her input when I started my own company and I trusted her in this situation as well.

I had her on my mind a lot because she had come to visit Mom and this was right after the doctor said no more visitors for more than five-minute stretches. They were trying something new at that time and it just happened to be that Cousin Sarah and her husband, Ed, were the next two people to show up. I felt horrible having to tell her the new '5-minute rule' when they had driven over an hour to be there in the first place. I spent the next few days sulking to myself about having to be such an arse towards her. I couldn't take the guilt so I picked up the phone and called her. This was a few days prior to the Sunday Rosary that I placed the call.

I confided in her how scared I was, but that I was trying to keep a brave face for everyone else. She offered to bring food over and I gladly accepted, having eaten her cooking before, I knew how amazing it was! However, with everything going on I completely forgot

I had accepted her offer and headed from the hospital to the soccer stadium. She called and let me know she was on her way to drop off the food and I was embarrassed because I forgot. Afterwards I got a call from Emily saying that half my family showed up at our house to come together and rally around.

It was at this moment that I instantly thought, 'oh crap, Sarah is showing up with food for four people and there is going to be over 20 people at my house.' Thinking fast, I told Emily to order pizza for everyone and save the Sarah gift for when I got home. As it turned out to be, like Jesus taking two fish and loaves of bread, and making enough to feed everyone. Sarah, somehow, someway did the exact same thing! Emily explained it to me later that night when I got home, apparently Sarah brought enough food to feed an army and the pizzas weren't even needed. So, as I was at the soccer field meeting everyone for my new job, Emily and Sarah were back in North Olmsted feeding the masses. Emily and I often refer to it as "The Cousin Sarah Food Miracle." I cannot express our gratitude for this night and for her love in our family. She truly has been a guardian angel in my life that I will never take for granted.

Sarah's food miracle was one of many happening that weekend, and little did anyone know the biggest was yet to come. If we had thought we had seen it all, if we had thought nothing else could possibly happen, we were dead wrong. The biggest miracle, the biggest shock and the biggest sign that God has the final say in all of our lives, was still to come and about to happen!

CHAPTER NINE

Embraced by the darkness, I am losing the light, encircled by demons I fight. What have I become, now that I betrayed? I have been a slave to the Judas in my mind. Is there something for me to save in the wreckage of my life? I'm becoming a Judas in my mind... – 'Judas' lyrics by Chris Jericho, Fozzy (2019)

Judas in my Mind

Do you remember when we were younger growing up and at award ceremonies the celebrities and athletes would first thank God? Now, you almost never see that. Marriages aren't revered anymore. God isn't worshiped.

It's all sports and entertainment figures. We idolize them as a society and listen to what they say and care about, or what they wear and do. No one is happy anymore and they resort to drugs, sex and possessions. So now people obey because they have nothing else to believe in. It's wrong. Society needs something real to believe in. Not fake, not manufactured, not even slightly altered, real! That's why the hashtag of Fight Maria Fight continued to take off and give people that organic and very real thing to believe in.

May 1, 2017 will forever be the darkest day of my entire life. It is one I remember vividly, but with great sorrow and pain. Three years later I still haven't talked about it in detail until this very moment. It is a day that will forever haunt me in my memories. Everything I fought for was gone, and the chances of getting any of it back, seemed about 100,000,000 to 1.

Up until now, you have sat through eight chapters of "stories." Some funny, some not so much but all with a purpose. The entire book is about to happen in the next couple of chapters. This is the "climax," if you will; the main reason you cracked this book open in the first place. That much I'm sure of. I'm about to tell you things I thought I would never tell anyone. Things that have taken me years to comprehend, and I'm still not sure if I do.

I woke up that morning and like the previous 12, checked my phone for news of any kind. To my shock, there was news this time. It was from Don and it was good. He got word early that they were lowering the vent down to 60% as Mom had a tremendous improvement over night. Maybe saying the rosary helped?

I quickly threw on my clothes and was about to bolt for the hospital when I received a follow-up message from Dad telling me to go to work. So, I did what I was told and went to work. I was going to respect his wishes in any situation. At about 12p.m. that day I got a message from Don saying they were moving the vent pressure down to 50%. This was incredible, this meant she was doing half the breathing on her own and showing huge signs of improvement.

This woman was left for dead not even two weeks ago, and here we were with her fighting like hell to stay alive. She was fighting for life and proving us right for not giving up. The clock was ticking as she only had a limited amount time left on the vent but she was proving it wasn't over with yet.

I called Don because I wanted to make sure I was understanding everything I was reading. His words to me on the phone sent chills up my spine with excitement and utter shock. I had been preaching for weeks that everything would be okay and she would beat this, but when you hear someone else say it *actually* happened, it is one of the most surreal feelings. It was now 2p.m. at the time of this call and Don proceeded to tell me the news we prayed for nonstop. They were taking Mom off the vent. Somehow, someway in the last 24 hours her body responded to everything they were doing, and the prayers around her. She was going to make it! She was going to play with her grandkids again, by God she was going to make it!

As much as I preached this to everyone who would listen, the Judas in my mind never truly let me believe it. The Judas in my mind had this little dark secret voice telling me I was wrong, and I was giving everyone false hope. The Judas in my mind never let me truly believe, even though I wanted to badly. I knew what I felt in my heart and what I was saying out loud, and I knew what the inner most dark places of my mind were saying as well.

I told Don to let me know the second she was off the vent and what the next steps were. The seconds turned into minutes, and the minutes turned into hours that felt like a damn eternity. Before I knew it, it was 4:30p.m. and time for me to punch out and leave. As I was walking to my car, I was about to call Don when he texted me. 'Mom is off the vent, get here and let's celebrate.' Two seconds later I got a text from my Aunt Anna, 'she made it, time to celebrate, get your ass here!' It was just one message after another. I even heard from a kid who I hadn't spoken to since high school saying that he saw my brother's post on Facebook just now and that he was crying. It was nuts.

The 45-minute drive from Fairlawn, Ohio to Fairview Hospital took 90 minutes that day because of the five-car pileup on I-77 before I got to the I-480. I mean, it had been weeks of hell, why not 45 extra minutes.

Emily had already been there with Abbie and my cousin, Frances and called to fill me in while I was stuck in traffic. Apparently, Mom had a light mask on but was sitting up and appeared to be fine. I guess people flooded in and out and she was talking to all of them as if nothing had even happened. Emily called me emotionally to share her excitement. She also let me know that Mom looked great but she had to get home to relieve the sitter. Our next-door neighbor, Gina, stepped up that day to help us out because Carrie had to leave early to take senior photos. Gina was just another saint in our lives.

By the time I got there, things were different, very different and not at all what I hoped to walk into. After being flooded with messages of family members celebrating, I walked into the room and didn't see a woman sitting up talking, I saw my mother struggling to breath. It was scary as hell, and I instantly got worried she was about to "code." This is slang for when your heart stops and you are pretty much dead. Dad was the only one there and he was panicking too. Doctors and nurses were flooding the room to check on her and trying to get her breathing to calm down. Her heart rate was racing and she was struggling to breathe. I knew instantly, and I mean instantly, we were headed for bad news. From one look, her turning white and gasping for air, I knew something terrible was about to happen.

Dr. Salem yanked Dad and me out of the room and gave us some grim news. Apparently, they felt they may have taken her off the vent too soon because she was struggling. Dad and I pleaded with the doctor to give her time. We asked him to let her rest with the mask on for a few hours and see if she could regulate her breathing. Dr. Salem who was amazing during this entire process, granted our wish and agreed not to put her back on the vent just yet. He said if we went home and allowed her to rest through the night with no visitors that he would give it a shot. Dad and I agreed, said a brief goodbye to Mom and left with hopes of no phone calls coming with horrible news.

It was a weird feeling walking back to our cars in the parking lot. We got what we prayed so hard for, but it still felt like a defeat in that moment. I gave my Dad probably the longest and hardest hug I have ever given him. I told him a line that I firmly believe to be true in any aspect of life, 'it's always darkest before the dawn.' I sat in my car for a good 20 minutes before I pulled out of the parking bay. I just sat there and stared out of my window. I was exhausted and just kept thinking over and over again about how much Mom loved her grandkids. For years and years that is all she ever talked about: how bad she wanted grandchildren. She now had three amazing ones and may never see them again.

It was the love of her grandchildren that kept her alive. I knew it in my soul that her love for Matthew, Maggie and Madelyn would be stronger than any diagnosis that a doctor could draw up. I believed in the power of her family around her, her friends like Camille, Cathy, Jenny and Sue, just to name a few. All the poor people she gave haircuts to at all the charity functions she helped with and even organized.

Having seizures for so many years of her life wrecked her brain in many ways, but it didn't wreck her heart. That alone is what kept her pushing, and me pushing for her. As I've said many times in this book, it was her love of her grandchildren combined with the fact that God wouldn't take a third child from my Grandparents. It may seem like silly reasoning, it may seem like fool's gold, but I refused to believe any different. Even if the Judas in my mind kept telling me, 'she is going to die, give up already!' Damn that Judas in my mind, damn him! No matter how hard I tried to block it out, it was there and getting louder by the moment. As my family celebrated, she was off the vent, I knew better. For a drive that took me 90 minutes to get there, I couldn't have been at the hospital nine minutes. But it only took nine seconds to know Mom was in big time trouble.

As I drove home, I once again took the long way, past St Patrick's where they went to church and where we were baptized. I drove past my boyhood home before it was floored into a field. Drove past my Grandparents' old street, the whole deal. There was just something about those old memories I kept going back to, which kept me sane. Eventually, I got back to North Olmsted and had to stop off at the store before going home. As I drove down Lorain Road, I saw the sign at Malley's Chocolates. In big bold letters it said, '**Fight Maria Fight**.' I used to work there in high school and recalled how they would always put birthday wishes for their younger customers up on the huge sign. The day before on my way to soccer, I had stopped in and requested that it be done.

Clara Malloy, the longtime manager, was nice enough to agree to do it, and even waived the cost after I explained to her what was going on. It felt amazing to see it in big bold letters like that too. '**Fight Maria Fight**.' As I got out of the car to go inside and thank her, I suddenly got a pit in my stomach, and something told me not yet. As if, the worst was yet to come. I can't explain it other than I just had this feeling; a really bad one at that. I got back in my car, not wanting to tempt fate, and drove home.

A few seconds after I pulled into my garage, Don, Abbie and Mathew pulled in behind me. It was so nice to see my nephew, Matthew. I really missed him and cherished our time together. I hated having to see him under these circumstances, but it was much needed! They were coming over to watch Game One of the NBA Eastern Conference Semi Finals between our beloved Cleveland Cavaliers and Toronto Raptors. Don had stopped off for pizza and wings and it looked as if we had several reasons to celebrate the big night.

I waited until I greeted Matt and gave him a giant uncle sized hug and made sure to let them visit for a quick minute before I pulled Don aside. I informed Don that Mom was struggling badly when I was there and the chances of her going back on the vent were strong. Don thought it would be a good idea for us to visit Dad as he and Mom only lived seven houses down. I agreed and we told our wives we were headed down to check on Dad. Upon arrival at Mom and Dad's you could tell quickly Dad was a worried mess. It was the most worried and stressed I had seen him throughout this entire ordeal.

It was funny though, because despite the seriousness of the situation, he was sitting there chomping on this giant goose liver sandwich. It was disgusting but for whatever reason he loved that kind of stuff. As Don and I tried not to gag, Dad was going to town like it was Thanksgiving dinner. It was just nice to see him eat as he had been losing weight since all this started. But man, oh man, was that thing gross.

We both tried to comfort Dad and remind him how far Mom had come, and that she was stubborn. She was a fighter and that 24 hours from now, things may look much better. We re-assured him that without any of us there, she would rest and continue to get better. The good news was she was off the vent and that was all that truly mattered. It was right after that his phone rang. It was Dr. Salem.

She was going back on the vent. Insert whatever cuss word you may choose, as pretty much all of them were said in that moment by all three of us. Dad bolted for the door and before we could blink, he was on his way back to Fairview Hospital. Don and I sprinted home to grab my car and get up there ourselves. Matt and Abbie left for her parents and I told Emily to be on standby. As Don and I floored it up to Fairview ourselves, we tried to keep the mood light by joking around about how disgusting Dad's dinner choice was.

As we pulled through the emergency gates at Fairview Hospital all I could think about was the last time I had to rush to Fairview. It was September 10, 2016 and I was rushing from covering UFC 203 to see my daughter Madelyn being born. This time around, I wasn't rushing to the hospital for the birth of a daughter, but rather, the possible death of a mother. I cannot begin to tell you the pain.

If I thought driving there was scary, and witnessing my Mom on a vent for 10-plus days was painful, that was nothing compared to the next five minutes of my life that have lived with me every day since. They have stuck with me every minute of every day and never leave the darkest corners of my mind. There's a good chance they never will.

As Don and I parked the car, my phone was ringing and it was Dad. He must have sped there because he was already in the room and I could hear chaos in the background. He was crying. It is the first, last and only time I have ever heard or seen my father cry – hard. He was screaming, 'get here now, Mom is about to die.'

I froze dead in my tracks, instead of running faster towards the entrance, I froze. I felt vomit start to rise from my stomach up my throat and couldn't contain it. I've struggled with nerves and anxiety my entire career in sports journalism. To the point that sometimes I break out in anxiety attacks as I pull into stadiums. This was different. This wasn't nerves. It wasn't anxiety; it was intense pain. I never want to see my Dad have to go through that again. Bottom line, above all else, that is a pain I wish I can remove from his life to the point he never has to endure it again. A memory that will never go away. No number of pills, alcohol, exercise, talking, or anything will make that go away. My Dad spent 30-plus years worrying about me, and I will now spend the rest of my life worrying about him.

I snapped out of it and ran after Don who was about a good 25 feet ahead of me. He actually got to the elevator before me and held it until I hopped on. Every second seemed like an eternity. When we got to the ICU Dad was signaling us to keep coming down the hallway past the entry doors that happened to be open. It was like a third base coach telling the runner to round third and score.

Don was ahead of me as we came down the hallway and Dad grabbed him as they headed for a meeting room at the end of the hallway with some orderly. For whatever reason, I stopped and didn't go with them. To this day I don't know why I stopped, but something told me to. Was it the Judas in my mind? Was it fear? I'll never know.

I was in front of Mom's room where I heard a ton of chaos. I pulled the curtain back because the door was still open. There must have been five to eight people in there with her, or so it seemed. My mind was racing. Nurses, doctors, everyone in blue and white and working to keep her alive. Why the door wasn't locked, I'll never know, maybe they don't lock. It doesn't matter now.

I saw my mom laying there completely naked as they took turns shocking her with the pads and beating the crap out of her trying to get a heartbeat. I looked at the small white computer screen next to her bed, one that I studied like a SAT test booklet for two weeks straight. It was no longer beeping or making any noise at all. It was a simple straight line that wasn't moving. Mom was dead.

To this day I have played it over in my head at least 1,000 times and no matter how I re-live it, I can never understand why I stopped and looked. Maybe God wanted to spare Dad and Don from that pain? Again, I'll never know.

I stood there frozen at what I was seeing. Dad no longer had his wife of 40 years. My Grandparents had lost their third child and my own children just lost their Grandma. As I stood watching in the hallway, I felt Donald yank my arm and scream at me to come in the closed-door room they were holding us in.

They brought us into this room with windows and a closed door. I realized quickly it was a conference room and it would become a room we spent the majority of the next 18 hours in. We then sat in there for at least 25 minutes before anyone came in and saw us. Dad explained to Donald and me that when he got there, they wouldn't let him in the room because they were trying to place Mom on the vent and had to do it with closed doors. All he knew was that it didn't go well and they asked him to go in this room we were currently sitting in because Mom wasn't doing well in the process. This was told to him by one of the nurses.

I quickly figured out that he only knew half the story, and it wasn't my place to tell him the other half. I felt that it was a few more minutes until a doctor walked in and told us what I already sadly knew, Mom was dead. I didn't want to rob my Dad of those few minutes of still believing Mom was alive. I wanted him to have that last bit of hope before the grim news.

Finally, after what seemed like days, but was only a few minutes, the doctor walked in. I fully expected him to say, 'Mr. McKee, your wife has passed away.' There wasn't anything else he could possibly say. I saw it with my own two eyes, she was dead! Except she wasn't as the doctor began to explain.

Dr. Salem cleared his throat and said the following, 'We tried putting your wife back on the vent because she was showing signs of not being able to breath on her own and was a heavy risk to code. As we began the process her throat was too swollen and it became nearly impossible to get her back on the vent. We used the smallest vent tube possible, but it still didn't work. During the struggle she went into full cardiac arrest and died on the table.'

I thought that was it, I fully expected my Dad to lose it, but then the doctor continued and took things to a place I never saw coming. He put us in a scenario so tough, I wouldn't wish it on my worst enemy. Dr Salem then said, 'We were able to save her, get her back on the vent and re-establish a heartbeat and pulse.'

I quickly yelped, 'Wait, what, she is alive? Is she okay?'

The doctor went on to say, 'She was gone for 17 full minutes with no oxygen, no brain waves, no anything. She died for 17 minutes before we got her back. However, because of this she may have to spend the rest of her life brain dead on a vent unless you opt for the tracheotomy, and even that is far from a sure thing.'

The options became clear: either get her the tracheotomy which would have kept her alive, or, let her stay on a vent for 10 more days until she was taken off it, and died. On the tracheotomy she would have been a vegetable the rest of her life because of the 17 minutes without oxygen. It would still not *even* guarantee she would be able to stay alive on the "trake."

Or, do the humane thing and let her go as soon as everyone had a chance to say goodbye. I was already against that because that meant giving up. However, as badly as I opposed that option, it would be the one that became imposed by just about everyone.

The vent was now doing 100% of her breathing again, and it was clear that the miraculous comeback she made last time was absolutely impossible to happen again. It was over. No matter how hard I didn't want to face it, the Judas in my head won.

As Don picked up his phone to dial Abbie, alerting her to get to the hospital ASAP, I realised I now had some calls of my own to make. The first, second and third were not to Emily. She would be dialled at the end as I knew I had some work to do quickly.

Call one was to Aunt Franny to alert the entire DeLuca family to get to the hospital to say goodbye to Mom's unconscious, lifeless body – not for her, but for them. I called Franny and once I said the words, 'I have some very horrible news,' she screamed, 'no!' and handed the phone over to Uncle Matt. I delivered the message to him and knew he wouldn't fail to get it to everyone else.

The second call was to my best friend, Dave Murphy. As spoken about in the last chapter, he was my lifelong friend who I would move mountains for if I could. He is loyal, dependable and in a lot of ways, a hero to me. There's nothing in this world I wouldn't do for Dave Murphy. My Mom loved him too, hell, my whole damn family loved him for that matter!

I asked Dave to go over to my house and sit with the girls so Emily could come to the hospital. Dave picked up on the first ring and immediately dropped what he was doing to leave for my house the second I asked him. He is that kind of man, all about everyone else, never about himself. A best friend and a brother!

The third call was to the other best Dave in my life, David 'Puka' DeLuca. He too, was much more than just a cousin; he was a brother and a best friend. After telling him what happened, I asked him to swing by the house and grab Emily. I didn't want Emily to drive emotional, and I knew I could trust Dave to get her there safely. As I figured, he was all about it and made no bones about throwing on his boots and going to pick her up.

The fourth and final call was to Emily. I wanted to wait until I had everything figured out before I called her. Less questions the better as time was fleeting. She was shocked but understood just how serious and close to the end it was.

After Don and I made the needed calls, it was right back to sitting in the room with Dad trying to get everything figured out. We were told that once both of our spouses arrived, the doctor would come back in and explain to everyone at once what exactly needed to be done.

As we waited, relatives began to flood into the waiting room of the ICU but even though we received the phone messages they were here, Don, Dad and I were not leaving that room. Don and I both knew we needed to be by Dad's side for the rest of the night. Dad broke down and threw his head in his hands and just started crying.

It was the most heartbreaking thing I have ever seen. I tried giving him his space and just letting him have that moment. It was tough though because at the same time you naturally want to comfort someone too. But what the hell do you say, 'we tried?' There's no fixing that situation, he had finally gotten that good news he wanted only for it to be followed by the worst news possible a few hours later. That my friends, is pure heartbreak. I lived it and know it well, nothing worse than thinking you have something beat and pulled off a miracle, only for it all to come crashing down moments later.

Here is where things get a bit dicey, and another reason it has taken me three years to go back to this dark place. After debating this in my own head over and over again, I'm placing this in the book and not taking it out because it is the story and needs to be told. Right or wrong, ego or not, it is the story. I understand this next part will get me in hot water with some, but the truth of what happened and went down next needs to be told accurately. I owe that to the readers, and myself.

Sitting in the room with Dad, I was led to believe that it was over. There was no chance in hell that Mom could possibly make another comeback and that we had to pull the plug. We had to do the right thing, respect her do not resuscitate (DNR) and let her go. This is what I was being told and given little chance to give input. I just sat there and listened to what we thought to be the only option.

Emily and Abbie arrived and entered the conference room. Then shortly after, my cousin Gena and Tony who were the two oldest cousins in the family and in the medical field. Dad trusted their opinion and wanted them in there. I was totally fine with it and so was Don. Quite frankly, even if we weren't, I wasn't going to tell Dad no to anything at that point. Emily and Abbie were both crying hysterically, as Don and I just sat there stunned that this was *actually* happening. Dad kept his head buried in his hands and I just kept rubbing his back and shoulders, trying to tell him it wasn't over yet.

Dr. Salem walked in and laid down the gauntlet for the room. The options weren't changing, it was basically unplugging and die or go for the trake. He did say that the "trake" was the only option at a possible life. Albeit not a good one, a life. Also, that she could eventually come off the trake and live a somewhat normal life with a tiny oxygen tank and mask. Again, it was a very small chance, but a chance!

I asked the doctor at least eight questions about each option and more so how the trake would work. I simply don't believe in taking anyone from this Earth in any format. No matter the situation or condition, don't take a life. No death penalty, no abortion.

Cousins Tony and Gena spoke first and their biggest concern was that Mom wouldn't be a vegetable or suffer. It was clear their compassion and heart wanted Mom at peace. I understood that and I respected that. They are both incredible people and their love for Mom is remarkable. They lost their own mother, my Aunt Joe, less than seven years before that and had every right to be bitter and cold. Instead, they were the exact opposite and it was clear their heart was in the right place. Don agreed with them and it seemed like a done deal. Mom would be taken off the vent and go up to heaven shortly after.

There was only one problem. I didn't want to give up, and no number of stone-cold facts were going to sway me. I could be a real stubborn pain sometimes and I wouldn't give up, not yet. Not until every single option was exhausted.

I pleaded with Dad and everyone else in the room that we couldn't give up, not yet. I said these exact words, 'Dad, we have one bullet in the gun left, fire it! There is a reason she is still here, a reason she came back after 17 minutes, a reason the nurses and doctors ignored her DNR earlier tonight when she coded. You have one bullet left, God damn Dad, fire that fucking gun!' I then slammed my fist as hard on the table as I possibly could without breaking it.

I looked around and Don was fuming pissed, so was Emily, so was everyone in the room except the doctor. He just kept smiling at me, maybe he thought I was nuts, who knows? Don re-enforced that we were taking her off the vent and that was all there was to it. No one agreed with me and I was pissed.

Still it didn't matter, no matter what I said or how I pleaded, screamed and begged, no one was listening. Except for one person, Dad! He wanted to give it one more night, why not? He reasoned that there was no rush to make a decision right now.

He would publicly admit later on that he believed and hoped the Lord would take her that night after everyone left. Thus, taking her out of pain, and putting the decision in the only persons hands qualified to make it. Dad was right. We simply weren't qualified to make that call in that moment. We needed one more night to sleep on it and come back in the morning. His exact point was that if Mom was brain dead, we would take her off and let her go, if not then maybe we try something. Dad asked me to go address the family in the ICU room.

As I walked through the glass doors and saw everyone sitting there, I could tell that they were all anxious for news and looked horrible. It appeared as if they had just been through a 10-round fight with Mike Tyson. It was gut wrenching, but I knew what needed to be done, what needed to be said. I was about to tell Mom's siblings, her nephews, her nieces and worst of all, her parents that she was going to die. I couldn't give any false hope, I wanted too, but I had to be honest.

I began, with a lump in my throat, trying to stay brave, 'Less than two weeks ago we all stood here and prayed for a miracle together. I'm sad to say, we will not be getting that miracle. I thought we had; I truly believed we pulled it off, but we haven't. Mom's lungs are damaged now more than ever after cardiac arrest earlier tonight.

Right now, the vent is providing 100% of her oxygen and it doesn't appear that it can ever change. Dad has asked that we take the night to say goodbye, and by tomorrow morning, we will be taking Mom off the vent.'

After speaking and having to look at the heartbroken faces of my Grandparents, I was even more pissed off that we weren't trying the trake. I couldn't then, and I can't now wrap my head around it. Try every single option before calling it quits.

I told Emily to have Puka take her back home. She was still pissed at me for not giving up and making a scene in the conference room. I didn't care if this made her even madder. I wasn't going anywhere until everyone left. She gave me a little bit of grief but eventually understood my stance.

I didn't want to talk to my cousins. I didn't want to talk to Don. I just wanted to sit in the corner of Mom's room and spend as much time with her as I could. One by one her sisters, nephews, nieces, brothers and parents filed through to say goodbye. It was so strange because the more people who came in the room, my Mom would open her eyes and make motions with her face. Her hands were tied down so she couldn't rip out the tubes in the middle of the night and commit suicide. But she could still shake her head up and down as people asked her questions.

She had zero medicine in her, and wasn't doped up to the point where she was knocked out. She was wide awake and fully aware of what was going on. As people were talking to her, she was responding with a series of nods, winks and mouth motions. A person who is brain dead, can't do any of that, but again no one listened. It wasn't even that they weren't listening, I think it was just trying to cope with reality and that is fine. But as Puka walked in one last time to say goodbye with Emily, I pointed it out to him and he thought the same thing I did. Yes, the machine was breathing for her, but she clearly knew what was going on. Why not just keep her on the vent until her lungs heal up?

Don and Abbie took Dad home after we convinced him he needed to go home and try to rest before what would be the hardest day of his life. He understood and left, although I was wise enough to realize there was no way he was going to rest. The last person in the room with Mom and I was Gena. She was taking this very hard as she had already lost her mother, and now it appeared certain she would be losing her oldest Aunt as well. Her and Mom were close and she was extremely emotional. By this point the excitement of the night had finally caused Mom to pass back out so Gena and I just sat there for hours talking, neither wanting to leave.

At about 4:30a.m., we both got up and left. Kissing Mom goodbye and letting her know we would be back in the morning. Gena had promised to stop up one last time before we took her off the vent. As we walked to the cars, I asked Gena if she had one last chance to save her own Mom on her death bed with some miracle pill, would she have done it? She said, 'No.' Explaining that it was God's will and not hers. It made a ton of sense and for the first time in weeks I felt at peace.

As I began to pull out of the parking lot, I realized I had left my parking slip in Mom's room. I quickly parked my car and made the long walk one more time. Down the white hallways, to the clear elevator, to the ICU waiting room, through some doors past a busted coffee machine to her room.

★★★

As I approached the room, one of Mom's nurses was standing outside of it. I had shared a lot with this nurse over the last two weeks and we became close. Nightly talks about our families and lives to the point where I felt like I really knew her. Her name was Grace, and as it turned out we had kids the exact same age, and we only lived minutes from each other. In my mind, it was almost like God sent her because she was the nurse who could relate to me, match my intensity, but also had a softer side and knew how to communicate even bad news in a gentle and caring way. She was incredible. She explained how she never really cried at work because working in the ICU desensitizes you at times, but that she felt the outpouring of love from family and friends for Mom, and that it overwhelmed her. This nurse began pulling for Mom and was also devastated that she coded. She had a tear in her eye, and I gave her a hug, but quite honestly, I did it because I needed a hug at that point too.

Grace started working in the medical field as a nurse in August of 2013, right before her first child was born. She accepted a job in the Fairview hospital ICU in December of 2013. In January of 2021, nearly 4 years after Mom coded, I spoke with Grace about everything that happened. Here below are some excerpts of that powerful conversation that day.

'I feel that the ICU was for me because it is the exact intersection of things that I'm good at. Seeing what is wrong, what could go wrong, and responding. You have to be ice cold under pressure. The flip side of the ICU is the large amount of end of life care we have to do. You have to make sure everything you are doing is correct. There is no room for error and you must also advocate for your patients,' said Grace.

She went on to say, 'I work really hard not to take patients home with me and try to call everyone by their last name. This makes it easier on me to be present with my kids when I get home. It's a way to create a wall so I can keep coming back and doing it again. Maria was different and so was her family.'

While this was true, she goes on to explain why it was different when it came to the McKee Family, 'I was blown away with the support for Maria. The ICU is a really scary place and when

I first met Maria, I didn't think she would make it. I didn't have a good feeling. I was stunned by the family and community support she had.

I was amazed by the love her family had for each other. I don't always see that. I see yelling and tension and stress. The amount of people who genuinely *loved* Maria, her husband, her kids, it was incredible. This family is doing it right! Whatever they have, should be a goal!'

While end of life care is a major part of what nurse Grace does, and she realizes it is a portion of her job, she explains why this time was different. 'Patients who get into your heart are always different. Your family was so kind to the staff, and each other it was hard not to pull for you. I was really pulling for you guys hard. It is not that I don't pull for everyone, but there was just something special about you guys.'

***

It was clear, it was either tracheotomy, miracle, or death. We had used our miracle once to save Don eight years prior, and Mom would never want the "trake" no matter how hard I pulled for it. It was time to go home.

By this point, it was now pushing 5a.m., and we had agreed to meet Dad, Tony and Gena back up at the ICU at 8a.m. There was no point of going home to sleep, so I went to a 24-hour restaurant called, Café Sal's. This choice was ironic for two things, one being that it is directly across the street from Malley's Chocolates & Ice Cream. So, as I sat in the booth at cafe, and I could see the bright sign of '**Fight Maria Fight**' glowing in the dark night. Almost like the cruel boot of defeat kicking me in the gut with every bite of food and every sip of coffee. I just kept staring at the sign, choking back food and guzzling coffee with the plan to stay awake.

This was more than a family member being sick, this was the past, present and future mixed into one giant ball of failure. As I sat there crushing one cup of coffee after another, I got more and more pissed. I was a failure: Mom wasn't going to make it and it was my fault. And then all those people who refuse to have faith would have another reason to mock it.

Dad was always there to make things better. The first day of my first apartment, the cable guy showed up and only installed cable in one room. He was about to leave when Dad asked him to step outside for a moment. A few minutes later the cable guy was back and I suddenly had cable in every room. What was I supposed to do? Ask Dr. Salem to step outside and then two minutes later Mom would have a giant tube stuck in her throat to help her breathe?

Bottom line, we were screwed, Mom would be dead within hours. Or so we thought…

CHAPTER TEN

Jesus said to her, 'I am the resurrection and the life. The one who believes in me will live, even though they die; and whoever lives by believing in me will never die. Do you believe this?'

'Yes, Lord,' she replied, 'I believe that you are the Messiah, the Son of God, who is to come into the world.' – John 11:25-27

The Miracle

Every time I closed my eyes, I saw the fear and sadness in my family's faces. Every time I blinked, I saw another moment that would never happen again with my children playing with Mom. Every time I took a deep breath, I felt guilty because it wasn't one I could take for her. As the moments came to a close, and the end drew near, nothing short of a miracle from God himself would save Mom.

Upon arriving home around 7a.m., I saw Bev outside walking her dog. Bev was our incredible next-door neighbor who had been watching Maggie and Madelyn every Wednesday since birth. She quickly asked me for the latest on Mom as I guess Emily had called her during the mayhem the night before. I told Bev the grim news that we were only hours away from having to take Mom off the ventilator and pass away into heaven. She offered to sit with the girls so we didn't have to take them to the ICU, thus being able to all go in the room with Mom when she passed. Kids were allowed in the waiting room, however, not the actual rooms of the patients. It was generous and much needed as we had no other options that day. It amazed me how people stopped their routines to help us.

I went in and woke up Emily who was already stirring. I then laid down on the floor with my head in my hands and just prayed for a miracle. I knew it seemed crazy, but despite everything, I wasn't ready to quit. I just kept reasoning that if her lungs were getting better less than 24 hours earlier, what had changed? I fully understood she had massive cardiac arrest, but she came back. Why did she come back? It had to have meant something. The whole argument of her being brain dead and on a ventilator the rest of her life was also nonsense to me. After what I saw last night, she clearly wasn't brain dead. If anything, we were back to square one of healing her lungs.

I was born a very competitive person and have never lost that trait. I despise losing. Emily gets angry at me sometimes because I don't let our two daughters win at board games. I make them earn it. It is what drives me, to win, to succeed, to watch hard work pay off and never accept no for an answer. A big part of this is also accepting faults and realizing everyone has areas in which they could improve. I sadly know adults who are complete assholes now because their parents were too afraid to correct them or get them the mental help some of them needed. You can't shy away from things if you want change and improvement. You must have a move forward approach and willingness to sacrifice to win. Why were we quitting?

I don't take no for an answer, ever, in any situation without putting up one hell of a fight.

Who do you think I get that trait from? Mom! Now more than ever, that 'annoyance' to some, would become my greatest strength and perhaps only ally. As Emily and I headed to the hospital it was eerily quiet in the car. I mean, what the hell do you say? 'After we watch Mom die, want to swing over to Bob Evans for some hotcakes?' It was horrid, the worst 10-minute drive of my life. Thank goodness that Fairview Hospital was only that far away. I began to memorize each location over the last few weeks of making that drive several times a day down Lorain Road from Clague to the hospital.

As we walked in, Don, Abbie and Dad were already there in the waiting room praying. We asked Dad exactly how he wanted the day to go, and told him we would respect whatever his wishes were. Dad explained that he wanted a series of things to happen before we took Mom off the vent to rest at peace. He wanted Tony and Gena to come and say goodbye one last time as they were Mom's two oldest nephew and nieces. He then wanted Father Joe Pendekar to come back and once again give

Mom a last rights prayer (again). From there, he agreed that since Mom made little to no improvement overnight and that he believed her body had been through enough. He didn't want to watch her struggle any longer and was willing to accept the hand fate had dealt us.

Once Tony and Gena arrived, the doctor came in and spoke with all of us one last time. Each person would have a chance to say goodbye, and then we all had to clear the room as they took her off the vent. From there, immediate family only would be allowed back in to watch her take her last breaths and head up to heaven.

One by one, we went and said goodbye. When I was alone with Mom I whispered in her ear, 'It's time to shock the world. Get your butt up out of this bed and show everyone what you're made of. This is nothing, let's go already.' She just laid there motionless; she hadn't made a move since the night before when she grabbed that hanky.

We took down everything in her room as well. All the Fight Maria Fight signs people made along with the different trinkets people had sent for us to hang up. We also had the statue of Mary from Fatima in her room the entire time as well. It was as if we were boxing up for a move. It was so odd and very unsettling.

After we all said our peace with Mom, Father Joe Pendekar showed up for the last rights and that is when I saw divine intervention begin to happen. The kind of thing you read about but never expect to see happen in person until it actually happens. Father Joe had already read Mom her rights once during this ordeal a few weeks prior, but this time was different, very different. The first time around he spoke in English at a tone loud enough for us to understand what he was saying and pray along. This time he leaned in over Mom, almost nose to nose with her like you would see an umpire and a manager in a heated argument. His words very soft, and not in English this time, they were in Latin.

To this day, I have no idea what he said, but the intensity of how he said it was off the charts. Once done, he made a motion over her head, looked at Dad and left the room. I would bet all the money I have that he didn't give her the last rights that day, he prayed for a miracle.

Before we could instruct the doctors to unhook her, my Uncle Jimmy showed up. He was very spiritual and had special Holy Water with him. He had studied the Divine Mercy Secrets of Fatima for many years and knew exactly the power he had in that water. It wasn't normal holy water, it was from The Miraculous Springs of Fatima. This was the most powerful holy water on the planet. I would advise everyone reading this to look into the Divine Mercy Secrets and the power behind them.

Uncle Jimmy said a few words as he sprinkled Mom with the water. I knew what it was as both my Uncle Jimmy and Late Uncle Peter had shared some of the secrets with me growing up. I had no idea he had the water until then however. A powerful moment to say the least. He said a few words to Don and I, and he was on his way.

From there, things got very strange to say the least. A few of Mom's cousin's randomly showed up to visit. They weren't aware of what was about to happen and I knew I couldn't be upset that more people showed up. They didn't realize what was about to be done, so we had to tell them and it wasn't easy. I had told my aunts and uncles that I wanted nothing on social media until after she was gone and at that point everyone was to be contacted personally first. I didn't want my friends and Mom's friends finding out via social media that she was dead. That is news that needs to be delivered personally.

The wishes by Dad were that everyone would leave except his sons, and their wives when it came time to unhook Mom from the vent for good. Once everyone left, we had no choice, the grim end had arrived. Dr. Salem asked us one more time if we were positive this was the move to make. I wanted to scream, 'No, cut her throat and try the trake!' But, I knew that my protests would fall on deaf ears, so I didn't even bother.

Dr. Salem went on to explain that when you take a patient off the ventilator before their lungs were healed, only one thing can happen, they die. He went on to explain that because Mom went without oxygen for so long the night before, that she would pass quickly and be brain dead at the time of death. He said that it would happen quickly and we'd have a few moments before she took a last breath on her own and passed.

From there, the nurse came in and unhooked her from all the cords. She then laid motionless with only a tiny nose tube with a slight steam of air. We were told she was on high dosages of morphine and wouldn't feel anything. The nurse expounded however that it could take a few minutes, or a few hours, only God knew.

Dad kneeled next to the bed, and the rest of us gathered around it and each held a part of Mom's body. I kept staring at her, hoping for a miracle, telling myself over and over that it wasn't over and she was about to shock everyone. Even in these closing moments, I never truly felt like she was gone. People will tell you that they thought I was nuts, but there was just something telling me over and over again that it wasn't over.

Then, after several moments, the strangest thing happened: ABSOLUTELY NOTHING! Like George Costanza in his pitch to NBC for a TV show, nothing happened! Minutes turned into hours and before any of us knew it, we had been leaning over her bedside nearly three hours saying goodbye. Only one slight problem in that plan, Mom wasn't ready to say goodbye. In fact, she was ready for the exact opposite.

After a little while, she began talking back to us. Yes, this woman who was left for dead, who was supposed to be brain dead, began speaking. And this wasn't gibberish or struggled mumbling, but clear as day talk. Not only that, but she began to hold court, telling us all her wishes for us and our children. She even began assigning her clothing and jewelry by child and daughter in-law. This dialogue would go on for hours, and before any of us knew it, it was pushing eight o'clock at night. She had literally been laying there, "dying without oxygen or brain waves" all damn day! It was clear to me and anyone with common sense, she wasn't dying and Mom was going to make it.

That was not the dialogue we were being told however, and the plan was still for Mom to pass away and go up to heaven. We stepped outside of the room for a moment and spoke with Dad. He felt that the reason Mom was hanging on was because we were still there in the room with her. The nurse even agreed and explained that the stimulation in the room wasn't allowing her to rest and pass away.

My simple logic then and now is the same, that being, she wasn't dying. I pleaded with my Dad and Don both to get her water, a heavy dose of oxygen and let her body heal. Don was firm with me and kept telling me to respect Mom's wishes for the DNR. The only one who could request those things for Mom would be Dad. I had no power.

Dad wanted to stay with her one more night by her bedside on the low oxygen and see what would happen. He wasn't ready to let go, and I didn't blame him. I could see it in Dad's eyes that he was also in belief that we were seeing a full-blown miracle right in front of our eyes. The nurse explained that they would be moving Mom into a hospice room and start to treat it that way.

While I wasn't thrilled at this move because I still felt like it was giving up, it was a small victory to get Mom out of the ICU. Dad agreed, sent me and Don home and told us to stay by our phones. He wanted to be alone with Mom. We had no issues respecting his wishes and left him alone to be with Mom.

It's safe to say that I didn't sleep that night. The entire night I laid in bed thinking the same couple of things, 'get her food, get her a breathing treatment and let her live'. Repeatedly in my head I couldn't shake it. Why the hell are we giving up? She clearly wants to live. I mean, c'mon already! I became obsessed with it, and started looking up every single article on breathing treatments I could find. I didn't care for the idea of hospice because to me that was where people go to die. Clearly, I was wrong on that awful assumption and have since learned that is not always the case. My cousin Gena did a wonderful job explaining to me what hospice is, and it is not a death sentence every single time as I had thought. She is a hospice nurse and really helped me cope with what was going on.

The next morning came, and I hadn't slept a wink. I couldn't, who could? Who the heck goes to bed thinking, well, at some point tonight my phone will ring, and Mom will be dead? I had that thought all night and sleep simply wasn't an option.

Wednesday morning came around and I asked Emily to go to work. She understood my wishes and went to work. I then called over to Bev and asked her to sit with Madelyn. I knew if I could get to the hospital and Mom saw Maggie with me, that is all it would take to convince her and everyone else that Mom could make it. Mom adored Maggie, and Maggie idolized Mom. It would take two minutes of Maggie sitting on Mom's bed to put the finishing touches on this miracle. Silly logic if you will, but I didn't care, I was going for it! The logic was simple and if it worked, it would be powerful and prove what the heart can do.

After we parked in the garage, I called Dave Murphy to ask him a few questions about breathing treatments. He had done some of his clinicals in the emergency room during pharmacy school and I wanted to pick his brain on a few items. Not only did he have answers for me but his wife Kim, who is also a pharmacist, was a treasure chest of helpful information. She let me know about a patient advocate programme the hospital can offer, and how much they could help in my efforts to keep Mom going.

Health care advocates work closely with patients, their loved ones and other professionals working in the facility. The duties of a patient advocate include explaining financial information, taking complaints from patients and helping patients understand their medical rights. A patient advocate can guide you through the confusing maze of health care with caring sensitivity. They can focus exclusively on your needs and help you resolve concerns about the quality of your care, get the care you need, and ensure that your voice is heard and that you are included in decision-making.

They let me know that if I went in there and demanded a breathing treatment that it could happen. I took Maggie in my arms and entered that hospital on an absolute mission. There was no more waiting around for an answer. There was no more hoping for the best and expecting the worst. Mom was getting a breathing treatment that day or I was going to jail for making the largest scene in Fairview Hospital history. I didn't care how crazy I had to get; I was done planning a funeral.

Shockingly, things went a lot easier than I had anticipated. Mom was sitting up talking to a room full of people when we arrived. Both of my Grandparents were there, Dad, Cathy Wade and several of her siblings along with Don and his family of Abbie and Matthew. Mom was holding court and breathing well with those two tiny tubes in her nose. It was a direct contrast of what was going on less than 24 hours prior as we had been standing around her ICU bed awaiting her last breath and the great sorrow that would follow. This time, there were no tears, no heartache and no fear. All that was replaced with smiles and joy as Mom held Maggie in her arms it was like nothing had ever happened. I couldn't believe my eyes, the prayers and never say die mentality worked!

Shortly after we arrived, Dr. Salem walked in and saw Mom for the first time since she coded on Monday night. His eyes became the size of golf balls as I think he was stunned at that moment. You could see it written all over his face, a clear look that said, 'Holy shit! What am I seeing?' Could you blame him?

I knew I only had a few moments work with and had to act quickly. I asked Dr. Salem and Dad to both step outside of the room when he was done with this exam. I was convinced that if Dr. Salem explained to Dad what it would take for Mom to live, then he would listen. Sure enough, that is exactly what happened! I started off by asking Dr. Salem what the chances of getting Mom soft food, steroids for her throat and a breathing treatment were. He explained that all my Dad had to do was ask and it would be done. I then had Dr. Salem explain to him by doing this, the chances of Mom staying living and eventually healing completely were actually very good.

Dad's face lit up and for the first time in nearly a month, the light at the end of the tunnel was shining in our faces. Instead of allowing Mom to lay in a hospice bed until death, the new plan was getting her better and out of there within days. Dad agreed, and we suddenly had daylight in a nightmare!

The treatment began within minutes and I walked back into her room with a large smile on my face. We met with a hospice worker later that day, but by that time, my mind was made up and so was Dad's, we weren't planning a funeral, we were planning a party!

★★★

A funny side story comes from the mouth of one of Mom's best friends, Camille, 'I went to visit Maria that night bracing myself for the worst, and I walked out and said, "that Bitch is going to make it!"' Camille saw what Dad and I did, and the days of gloom and doom were over!

Thursday May 4th was Dave Murphy's birthday and I couldn't resist taping Mom, sing him Happy Birthday and send it to him! Had he and Kim not filled me in on the rights of a patient and what she was entitled to, who knows what could have happened. Emily and I brought the Zook in with us that night too, and it just seemed too good to be true!

By the time May 5th, also known as Cinco De Mayo, rolled around, the celebration was in full tilt! A lot of us went to visit Mom early in the evening. The breathing treatments were working, the steroids decreased the swelling in her throat, and she was able to eat apple sauce, and yogurt puree. It could have been Thanksgiving dinner for that matter! It all tasted like victory!

Cousin Fran hosted a party that evening for Mom's entire family. It turned into a celebration of life and not the kind you have to remember someone's life after they die. She had food and margarita's and you could see the relief and just pure utter amazement on everyone's face. We had spent nearly a month looking at each other in the ICU, praying for a miracle, and now we got one. It was just surreal. I wish I could explain it but some things can never be put into words. It was like hitting the lottery!

My Aunt Rose said to me that night how she had tried explaining to her clients at work everything that had happened that week and there was no way she could make it sound believable. My Aunt Franny told me that I should write a book about this all one day and I explained to her it would be impossible. Unless you saw all of it unfold, it would be hard to believe. Miracles can happen, and the biggest one I had ever seen just did!

★★★

Mom was set to be released from hospice on Monday, and the remarkable turnaround was soon to be complete. Cathy Wade, Camille Bensi, Jenny Ligetvari and Sue Hamer came over my parents' house on Saturday and spent six plus hours cleaning it from top to bottom. David and I used that opportunity to clean a lot of the junk out of the basement and attic as well. Mom had incredible friends. They were the best set of "second Moms" I could have asked for. Jenny was one of the sweetest human beings I haver ever met. She truly had a heart of gold and was also a professional cleaner which really came in handy that day. I cannot say enough great things about all of them!

The Divine Mercy Chaplet was said over Mom's bed at the hospice center on Sunday by old family friends from St. Patrick's Church. Cousin Tony showed up for that as well, and it was a beautiful ceremony. Everything appeared to be on the mend. Mom was healing. Dad was happy and the weeks upon weeks of terror and fear were finally over. Tomorrow, Mom would go home, and the pain would finally end.

Crazy enough, after leaving the hospital I had to head to another speech at a library. How wild was it that I had a speech at the start of this ordeal hoping Mom would make it, and then have another speech to book end the ordeal after she made it. The people of Berea Public Library were in for a real treat that day. I don't know if I could have been in a better mood, or had more energy than that afternoon.

As I drove home down Bagley Road, I passed by Baldwin Wallace's George Finnie Stadium. I didn't think much of it at the time, but that particular stadium would come to be one of my favorites' for a reason I will get too shortly. It would become a symbol of peace, happiness, and home.

I went to bed that night before 2a.m. for the first time in nearly a month, and it felt damn good. I slept like a baby. Victory had never tasted so sweet, not only did I still have my mother, but my girls still had their grandmother, my Dad still has his wife and my grandmother still had her daughter. That is all that mattered. It wasn't a victory for me, not by a long stretch. It was a victory for every person out there who prayed for a miracle and didn't get one. This time, it was granted and gave hope to thousands to keep their faith in the Lord.

One small thing I wanted to make sure I mentioned during all of this, between Carrie Pell, Bev from next door and Mandi from church helping out, we were never hurting for babysitters all of those Mondays and Tuesdays during this stretch. We were very blessed and I made sure to let Carrie Pell know that as I left for work that Monday morning. Little did I know, that was the last time I would ever see her beautiful face.

Work seemed to fly by as it just felt great to get back to normal, and I knew that by the time I got home, Mom would be home as well. I arrived home and shortly after so did Emily. I knew the hospice nurses had been at my parents. Everything was set up for in-home hospice as her recovery took place. As much as I wanted to take the girls with me, there was something that told me to go alone. Thank goodness I listened to my gut because minutes later a nightmare took place.

As I walked into my parents' house, I quickly noticed a few things. My cousin Libby Lombardo had set up a food chain for my parents, and meals were already showing up. I thought that was very nice as Libby is such a sweetheart who always puts others first. I also noticed my Aunt Franny and Cousin Connie were there visiting along with Don and Jenny Ligetvari. It was nice to see so much support for my parents. Before I could say a single word however, all holy hell broke loose as Mom went into a massive seizure. I couldn't believe my eyes (again) and just stood there still, amazed and horrified at what I was seeing. I had seen Mom seizure a plenty over the years, but this was different, much different.

All day I had been thinking and worrying that she was being sent home too soon, and this little 'mishap' almost convinced me as so. As Aunt Franny and Dad held her down, Don called 911. Moments later, the ambulance arrived and we were all on the way to the hospital. Yet again, a not so fun trip down Lorain Road to Fairview Hospital.

Answers at the hospital would come fast and furious this time around. As mentioned earlier, my Mom had brain surgery in the 80s but still required daily medicine to refrain from seizures. Well, it turned out that once they pulled Mom from the vent, they never put her back on her anti-seizure medicine because technically she was supposed to die. Dead people don't need medicine.

My Uncle Matt had arrived at the hospital and asked me for an update on Mom. I explained to him about her not getting the medicine she needed, and he was none too thrilled. I could sense he was thinking the same thing I was: someone had dropped the ball. Uncle Matt urged me to talk to someone and get a straight answer, so I did exactly that. I wrote everything down and spoke with a social worker later that day in person, face to face at Fairview. She promised me she would take care of it. Around 24 hours later, I received a call from the office of Toby Cosgrove, spoke with some woman and explained everything. In the words of Forrest Gump, 'that's all I have to say about that.'

Hospice or not, don't leave *anything* to chance. Starting that evening, Mom was back on her epilepsy medicine. Hospice is there to keep you comfortable as you slowly die, or slowly heal. It doesn't mean you shouldn't be getting your medicine.

Mom was released the next day, and take two went a lot better than take one. She wouldn't return to the hospital for nearly 19 months. The nightmare was finally over and the greatest summer ever was about to begin.

CHAPTER ELEVEN

'Science investigates; religion interprets. Science gives man knowledge, which is power; religion gives man wisdom, which is control. Science deals mainly with facts; religion deals mainly with values. The two are not rivals.' – Martin Luther King Jr.

'Into the Sunset'

2017 was the greatest summer of my life with some of the happiest memories I will ever have. Everything seemed to fall into place. After weeks of non-stop stress, things just started going right. Carrie Pell sent us two of the best sisters anyone could ask for in babysitters. The two young girls were Olivia and Serena; a pair of sisters from Strongsville that Maggie and Madelyn took to instantly. They took over watching the girls on Monday and Tuesdays and were a perfect fit!

Mom continued to heal slowly but surely and because of Libby's food train, which she set up on Facebook, my parents didn't have to worry about a single meal the entire summer. People from all over Ohio and even as far as West Virginia and Pennsylvania showed up with food at times. It was one of the most touching things I've ever been blessed to see.

Best of all, was the fact that Matthew didn't leave to head back to North Carolina until the first week of June. We had him for a month straight, and you better believe I made sure to see him every single day he was home, complete with several sleepovers. He came over for Cavalier playoff games, and plenty of wrestling nights and wiffleball in the backyard as well. It was just incredible and memories I will forever cherish.

Even the fireworks on the fourth of July seemed better that summer. Helping matters that night were my parents asking to let Maggie have a sleepover. I recall them coming over to pick her up and just staring at Mom in the passenger seat. Deep down inside, I still couldn't believe she was alive, let alone sitting there in my driveway as Dad loaded Maggie in the car.

Speaking of Dad, my goodness did he and I have some fun that summer as well. The far back of my backyard was loaded with these pesky pine, oak and maple trees. We couldn't see Maggie when she wanted to play back there. Let alone they made our backyard much too dark. Our yard would often flood as every time we got rain, it would take a week to dry.

With all that being said, Dad and I decided to start taking them down one at a time. He took down the bigger ones with a chainsaw, while I took down the medium and smaller ones with an axe. It was great. I lost 30 pounds, had a great deal of fun and chopping down trees turned out to be great stress relief. I never suffered from PTSD because I think I got a lot of those bad memories out of my system with each chop of the axe.

By August, a backyard that once had 31 trees, was suddenly down to 14. I guess you can say we went a little crazy. However, we didn't receive any complaints from the people constantly stopping by our house for wood that summer. It was a camper and firepit paradise for many who swung by for the lumber.

The gig calling games with AFC Cleveland turned out to be as much fun and career advancing as I thought it would be. I learned a ton about the business that summer, and it would eventually lead to me starting my own company, 'Kee On Sports Media Group.' If that summer taught me anything, it was to bet on yourself and that is how Kee On Sports Media Group was born.

In the end, it all boiled down to the last week of summer, and the happiest of my entire life. While everything was going on with Mom's recovery, and all the drama and heartache that went into it. The biggest goal in my mind was Maggie's upcoming first day of school. Not only that, but Mom being in a position where she could join in the fun and comprehend the moment.

I would take Maggie on little trips to Forest Elementary School. This is where she would be going to school and I wanted her to get familiar with it. They had a giant playground outside of the building with plenty of things to do. I was a nervous rack on the inside because I wanted her to enjoy her first year of pre-school and not be scared. Thus, the trips were to make her comfortable and actually excited to get to go inside.

Our Lord just seemed to work in mysterious and great ways that summer because on our 3rd or 4th trip the janitor happened to be doing a walk through, and invited us inside to take a look. This was a huge thrill for Maggie and me both. It certainly helped calm the nerves. By the time the first week of pre-school rolled around, Maggie was chomping at the bits to start, and that is exactly what I wanted!

I'll never forget the final weekend of summer, and the beginning of school. It was the best time of my entire life and that is why I want to share it. After 150 plus pages of heartache and angst, I owe it to myself and you the reader to share this.

In a summer of signs, perhaps this was the biggest that it would all be okay. The day was August 25th and I took a half day at work to head home and help set up for Maggie's birthday party, the next day. We had a lot of excitement and a lot of people coming over. Mom and Cathy Wade were decorating the entire backyard while Dad and I set up tables and chairs.

It was beautiful out and the day just screamed happiness in my bones. Setting up for my eldest daughter's 4th birthday party and also just hours away from opening night of High School Football season.

Once decorated, I was headed to George Finnie Stadium, the home of Baldwin Wallace but also the Berea-Midpark Titans, who I would be covering that night as they hosted Strongsville. As I went through my pre-game routine talking with coaches and setting up my equipment in the box, I couldn't stop smiling. It was hard to even fathom what my family went through just a few months prior with Mom. And now, all of it, just didn't matter anymore, it was over and happiness was bursting through all of us.

The part of that night that stands out in my mind to this day, was halftime. My cousin Gena's daughter Gianna went to Berea-Midpark, and my cousin Gabriel played for Strongsville, so that means that Gena, Frances, her husband Mike, my Grandpa and my Aunt Anna were in the stands. I ran over at halftime and met them all in the crowd. We took a picture and it was the biggest smile I think I have ever had on my face that didn't require a wedding or birth. As they took the picture, I looked past the camera man and saw the lights, saw the band playing and the fans cheering. I saw happiness, I saw hope and at that moment, the last bit of pain that had been hanging on in my heart and soul, finally went away.

I have thought about that picture and that moment every single day since. When I'm sad, when I just want to give up, I think about that night and that picture. The deepest and darkest point of my life was finally over.

CHAPTER TWELVE

Maria Speaks

On January 13, 2021, my mother, Maria McKee, spoke on the record about what happened when she died and came back to life. It is transmitted here in written form, and in audio form with the Kee On Sports Podcast via Podbean.

> *Vince*: 'Upon checking into the hospital what are some of your earliest memories and did you feel like you would be walking out in a few days?
>
> *Maria*: You know me, I had to be really sick for me to agree to go to the hospital. When they told me, they were going to admit me, I asked your Dad to go home and grab my pillow and sleep apnea mask. I don't remember much until later the next evening when my nephew Tony was standing by my bedside begging me to allow the hospital to vent me. I told him no at first,

not remembering what Donny Joe [*her son Donald*] went through. I was so out of it at the time, I didn't remember much.

He begged me to go on the vent, and he eventually did talk to me into doing it. I agreed but reminded him and the doctors of my no resuscitation rule. That is the last thing I remember until I walked that tunnel that takes you into Heaven.

I laid in bed and didn't know what was going on. Sometimes I would open my eyes and see people standing by my bed, but not know what was going on as I thought it was just a dream. I do remember hearing Father Joe's voice at my bedside.'

Vince: 'What are some of your memories of being in the coma, waking up, coding, and then waking up again?'

Maria: 'When I died, I was walking with Father Joe, who was holding my hand. We were walking towards my deceased brother Peter, and deceased sister Josephine. Peter was cheering me on and telling me how much I would love Heaven, while Josephine was urging me to fight. Josephine begged me because she was positive my parents couldn't take losing another child.

The clouds then opened and there stood the Blessed Mother. I cannot put into words how beautiful she was. Father Joe then spoke and asked her if she was taking me. All she said was, 'no,' and I literally felt my body swish back to that hospital bed. I then heard voices but couldn't make them out or connect what had been going on.

The next thing I remember was talking to each one of my children and sharing with them my love. Sharing with them what I wanted them to have of mine, which is little to nothing, but at least something. The next thing I know I was walking hand and hand with Father Joe again up towards Heaven.

Peter was cheering me on once more while Josephine just kept begging me to fight. Father Joe grabbed Josephine's hand, and I grabbed Pete's as we walked this long tunnel again. This time the Blessed Mother Mary stood there in all her glory. She kissed my forehead and told me her and her son [*Jesus*] were very proud of me.

Father Joe once again asked her if she was taking me. Once again, the Blessed Mother turned to him and said, 'No.' The next thing I knew I was back in that hospital bed. I was back in the ICU and awake.

Vince: 'Why do you feel Father Joe was chosen to take that walk with you?'

Maria: 'Father Joe was from India and grew up as Hindu until he was 11 years old. In his neighboring city people praised Jesus, but also Mother Mary and he wanted to know who that woman was. He began to learn about the Blessed Mother.

He would eventually leave his family, the oldest of 11 children, for the seminary. He became dedicated to the Blessed Mother and worshiped her more so than any priest or person I have ever met. He taught me so much about her and when you were around him, you would feel her presence.

I think Mary chose Father Joe because of his love for her. It wasn't two weeks later that he came to me and thanked me for bringing him to his "Mama," which is what he called her. He described the walk we took and was able to repeat it word for word. That is when I knew it wasn't a dream because I didn't tell a soul. His mission was to help the sick and the poor and from that moment on he called me Lazarus.'

Vince: 'What do you feel saved your life?'

Maria: 'My faith and belief in God. The strength and love of my family that didn't want to lose me and fought to keep me alive. If every man loved their wife the way my husband loved me, they would be millionaires.'

EPILOGUE

'The best chance you have at success is to give yourself up to loneliness, fear nothing and work hard. You will learn that life is based less than you think on what you have learned, and much more than you think on what you have had in you from the beginning.' – Carl Jung

A Tribute to Rosemarie DeLuca: The Matriarch of a Dynasty

From tears of joy to tears of incredible pain. It was just this Tuesday night at her bedside, that Joe DeLuca told a story that made the entire room burst out in laughter, only to be followed by powerfully sorrowful tears.

For years Grandpa Joe would steal the room telling funny stories, and wise remarks one after another as a two-minute pre-meal prayer turned into a twenty-minute showcase of love and family. At the end of every story he would say, 'remember Ro?'

You see, 'Ro' was his wife of 66 years and the Matriarch of the Dynasty known as the DeLuca Family. 66 years of marriage. 19 grandchildren, 9 great grandchildren and endless love and pride.

This time, it wasn't the table that Grandpa ended the story with 'Right Ro?'. It was at her bedside, as she was taking her last breaths. He told a story and ended it the same way he always did, only this time Grandma would not answer.

Rosemarie DeLuca would make it through Tuesday as more than 85% of her family sat at her bedside taking turns weeping over her body. In my mind, her soul was already in heaven at that point.

Wednesday would be the last day her body would spend on this earth, but after 84 years on it, she had created a legacy that would last forever. To better understand it, let's start at the beginning.

★★★

Rosemarie Lombardo met her husband Joe DeLuca at John Adams. It didn't take long for them to fall madly in love, and even when Joe's family moved to Bay Village in his senior year of high school, Joe took every way of transportation to visit Rosemarie as much as possible and their love continued to grow.

It wasn't long after high school that they got married in April of 1953 and began what would become one of the greatest families of love and togetherness that anyone could ever dream of. Rosemarie was 18 and Joe was 19. Young love that would never die!

Only six weeks into marriage Joe got drafted into the army to serve in Korea, while Rosemarie found out she was pregnant with Aunt Josephine, their first of eight children. He would see her for the first time when the war was over and she was already born.

They would never be apart again as their message of love, God, and family would spread throughout everyone who came in their path. Rosemarie DeLuca was as close to a saint on this earth that you will find.

Think about it for a second. Changed diapers of all eight kids, all 19 grandkids and for more than 40 plus years, cooked Sunday meals to feed an army every weekend for whomever came over to the house. Again, stop and think about it. That's not just the eight kids and 19 grandkids she had, but most of their friends, boyfriends and girlfriends too.

Mrs. Rosemarie DeLuca was the utmost in everything she did, a wife, a cook, a homemaker, a mother, a grandmother, a friend, a sister, and a daughter. Her own mother died when she was 16 years old and she let that motivate her to be the best mother, grandmother and mother-in-law a person could ask for.

She was so beautiful, and Grandpa Joe would often say, 'when I look at her, I see the first girl and only girl I ever kissed. She looks every bit as beautiful as she did the day we got married.' When he looked at her, that is truly what he saw, each and every time, his bride! Every single time!

66 years of cooking meals, 66 years of doing laundry, 66 years of changing diapers, 66 years of holding babies, 66 years of kissing boo-boos, 66 years of going to little league

games, 66 years of going to concerts, award ceremonies, meeting first boyfriends, girl-friends, etc…

This woman did it all and never complained. You never knew when she was sick, she was so proud of her family that she would never miss a thing, no matter what kind of pain she was in.

She was labelled as a "homemaker." Well so what, look at her 84 years on this planet and her 66 as a "homemaker." I'm sorry, but she took that 'title' and made it a term that woman craved to hold.

She would often say, 'money can't buy what we have.' She never went on some fancy trip, never ate at a fancy restaurant. She didn't have to because her kitchen was the best bistro in the world and making food for everyone who walked through her doors was better than any vacation she could have taken.

She didn't care for material things, just treat-ing everyone around her with love and respect. She was accepting of everyone and everything as long as they were nice and God loving. She didn't care if you were black or white, gay or straight, from Parma or Pluto, when you came through those doors, you were family.

Can you only imagine how many butts sat on that couch? More than an RTA truck stop on a holiday weekend. Everyone was welcome, and I mean everyone!

Perhaps the thing that made her meals the most special over the years is that they were eaten without phones around. No one had a mobile phone and simply sat, ate and talked. It was family, it was love! Too often nowadays, people don't communicate. Lord knows that was never the case in the DeLuca home. Talking loudly for most people, was whispering to us. We are Italians, we are loud and proud!

There was no better showing of this when nearly 50 plus people crammed in her ICU room earlier this week to all say goodbye at once, and no one left her side until they had too. She was kindhearted and had the gentle touch that only a Grandma could have.

She was there for all of her grandchildren to be born, and most of her great grandchildren as well. In the delivery room most times. So many morning masses at St. Patrick's with her grandchildren. She would write in a journal daily, and never let her emotions towards any family pain cloud her judgement or weaken her strength.

Her having a journal encouraged me to have a journal as a kid.

Years later her and I would take turns writing to our pen pal cousin Jim in Montana. We'd often laugh at how similar his letters were structured compared to ours. It was weather, current events, something new, something old, and love every time.

She was always so proud of her grandkids, even when it was tough to be. Over the last year she kept telling me, 'Vince, now that you're getting famous, always remain humble, and watch out for those women because they are all going to want a piece of you.' It was so touching for multiple reasons.

One, I'm not famous, semi famous, locally famous or even to the point where people know who the heck I am at my own day job. And to, the women? That just makes me laugh. But in Grandma's eyes, I was a superstar, a champion at life. And just that encouragement helped with the 18-hour days and the long nights with little to no sleep.

I often said to myself, if Grandpa and Grandma can raise eight kids on a postal carrier's salary, then I can cover one more game this weekend or go another three months without a new pair of shoes, despite these ones having holes in them. Always put your children first and yourself last, always!

She taught me how to sacrifice. She taught me how to be grateful. She taught me that nothing comes easy but when you work for it, it is all that much sweeter.

She never missed a birthday as there was always a card in the mail. Even at 37 years old, I'd still get home and check that mailbox, sure enough, a card from Grandma every time.

It was tough because in her later years she couldn't eaten gluten. She'd get extremely sick if even a crumb touched the plate. And yet, her favorite meal was breakfast.

Now, she sits in heaven at the biggest breakfast table of them all, next to her son Peter who she lost in 2004, and daughter Josephine who she lost in 2010. Eating a piece of toast after piece of toast with butter! And not the crappy kind either.

This incredible woman lost two children. Twice in the last 15 years she had to bury adult children. A horrible pain I wouldn't wish on my worst enemy, and yet, she remained the pillar of strength throughout it all.

My Grandma Rosemarie DeLuca was so loving that she created a family based on God, love and family. I had thought that was the only way of life. It wasn't until I got older and started going around other families that I realized that wasn't always the case. Far from it in certain areas.

Again, she accepted every one of every walk of life. It didn't matter if you had two dollars in your pocket, or 200,000, she was going to love you and treat you like a king.

At DeLuca family get togethers, there may have been 50 plus mouths to feed at every get together, but you better believe that the food never ran out and everyone went home with a doggy bag filled with goodies. A staple that has never changed. And we all knew which drawer had the tootsie pops, and which cabinet had the Diet Caffeine Free Coke.

She never missed anything. She was always there in mind body and soul. And now, she may no longer be there in body, but I assure you she will be in spirit and soul. When she arrived in heaven on Wednesday night, her son Peter was waiting there with a giant empty bowl and spoon, just waiting for some pasta azul and some of that vintage homemade pizza.

Her daughter Josephine was also waiting on her, along with her mother, she lost at 16, as all three women finally got to meet all at once. 'Josephine, I'm so happy to see you again, please allow me to introduce you to your Grandma Lombardo.' She most likely said with tears of joy rolling down her cheeks.

★★★

Carl Jung once said, 'The best chance you have at success is to give yourself up to loneliness, fear nothing and work hard. You will learn that life is based less than you think on what you have learned, and much more than you think on what you have had in you from the beginning.'

I close with that quote for this reason, my beautiful Grandma Rosemarie DeLuca, never went to a single day of college, never worked a nine to five job, but she was the smartest person I have ever known. Simply because she understood what it really meant to be rich; what it really meant to be happy; she didn't need a book, she didn't a pulpit or a podcast to preach on. She just needed her family.

And now, she sits with the all the angels and saints, the ones on her holy cards all those years. Holding their hands, praying together and looking down upon us, looking down and smiling at the legacy and the dynasty that she built.

Rest in peace Grandma. We love you!

Lightning Source UK Ltd.
Milton Keynes UK
UKHW011133171221
395649UK00001B/19

9 781913 606664